CAESAR

and

GOD

CAESAR
and
GOD

The Priesthood
and Politics

ROGER VEKEMANS, S.J.

ORBIS BOOKS
Maryknoll, New York

Translated from the Spanish
by
Aloysius Owen, S.J.
and
Charles Underhill Quinn

© 1972, Orbis Books, Maryknoll, N.Y. 10545
Library of Congress Catalog Card Number: 77-179959
All rights reserved

Design and Production by PLANNED PRODUCTION, INC.
Manufactured in the United States of America

[iv]

TABLE OF CONTENTS

TABLE OF CONTENTS

[vii]

FOREWORD

In an age of secularization and "Death-of-God" theology, a theme such as the Church and the political world may seem to be of secondary, not to say marginal, interest. And it is certain that the whole of ecclesiology is in the process of being rethought even in its most basic aspects, and not merely from the point of view of the Church's relationship to the world.

This is substantiated in areas that go far beyond the purely theological, areas which touch on the most intimate aspects of life itself. It is enough to mention the numerous crises in the lives of priests today to see that what is at stake is not merely the question of the priest's place vis-à-vis the Church and society, but something much more profound: the credentials of the very essence of the priesthood itself.

Yet, however deep-rooted the post-conciliar unrest may be, and however acute may be the confusion accompanying it in many cases, there are subjects which may be somewhat obscured by the spectacular effervescence of today's world, but which nevertheless have not lost their fundamental relevance. In our opinion, the Church and the political world is one of them.

Fascinated or obsessed by the outbursts of a vocal minority, we may easily lose sight of the vast silent majority of faithful and priests who are undoubtedly troubled by fresh anxieties and aroused by new hopes, but who at the same time continue to be prodded by problems as old as Christianity itself. It is possible that with not a few of them, their relationship toward politics has become secondary, but for many this field continues to be pertinent and even essential.

On other continents, it may be that the so-called crisis of faith or of the priestly vocation has a different coloration, but in Latin America there seems to be no doubt that the political factor constitutes an important and crucial issue. If this is so, then the subject of this book is neither secondary nor marginal.

Even were it not so, and were the real problems those of radical secularization, our subject would still shed some valuable light on them, if only indirectly.

Our essay began with some jottings for a round-table discussion, but the objective demands of the theme required a much longer and tortuous course than had been foreseen. Thus, from a few simple notes there grew a book that became much more voluminous than I had intended, although it still has serious gaps and is therefore inconclusive.

However, these initial reflections may possibly be useful in crystallizing other more systematic and profound studies.

R. V.

I

THE CHURCH IN THE
WORLD

As a starting point, we shall adopt the "Church-World" polarization found in *Gaudium et Spes*. It will serve as a background upon which the basic theme of this essay will be projected and will lead directly into Part III: "Priesthood and Politics."

From the outset, it should be clear that of the four possible meanings of the word "world"—God's creative work taken as a whole, the world weakened by sin and in rebellion against its Creator, the whole body of men living on earth, man's established values and his concerns in the temporal sphere,[1]—it is only the last two that are relevant to our context: world-as-mankind and world-as-civilization.

Yet, every polarization, no matter how logically presented, runs the risk of setting up a dichotomy. The temptation to do so has always been present in the development of theological thought. The well-known polarities: earthly-spiritual, temporal-eternal, religious-secular, natural-supernatural, bespeak an ever-present danger that must be avoided. "Beneath such over-facile distinctions as these there is an underlying rudimentary image that implies that earthly, secular and temporal realities are merely 'opportunities' for the Christian to come into contact with them and save them, since in themselves they are indifferent, amorphous matter without intrinsic relationship to the kingdom of God. They constitute merely a provisional scaffolding for the 'supernatural' construction of the City of God."[2]

Of course, this does not mean we are to reject such distinctions, since they are grounded in the gratuitousness of grace itself. Were we not to acknowledge this gratuitousness, we should be postulating a demand in man himself for the supernatural, and thereby destroy the agapeic nature of God's love in Christ. However, since the divine *dilectio* fulfills an essential aspiration of human nature, and since in concrete existence there is in fact no such thing as "pure nature," but rather man redeemed from sin by the Son of God, it is indispensable that we carefully weigh the polarization we adopt so as not to fall into the trap of devising false conceptual "divisions." There is no doubt that the logical categories used succeed as pedagogical tools of analysis, as long as we do not lose sight of man's factual historicity. *Ab aeterno,* through God's free gift, man has been a supernaturalized being. Historically, man's being is not compartmentalized. The movement of his concrete existence is essentially one. In human activity, there is no area that is foreign to his eschatological destiny.

"It is correct to speak of laws and an organization that are proper to particular aspects of existence, even though existence itself is a unity. We must avoid the danger of thinking that there are separate or quite distinct areas, some of which would be outside the religious sphere . . . This is the dissociation, the exclusion of a dependence upon God, against which the Council warns us."[3]

THE CHURCH AND MANKIND

On first sight, this distinction can only seem fundamentally inadequate.[4] Mankind does not constitute a personal community or a fellowship, except through a life destiny and a vocation, which, as an *appel des valeurs,* is both a challenging task and a commitment. Indeed, revelation shows this *koinonia* to be the people of God, a people called by the initiative of God's grace—the supreme value—to establish a fellowship, the communion of saints. The specific form the call takes is "representative mediation," a fraternal service of man to man, based on the divine election which culminates in Christ who is the Alpha and the Omega, the *homo principalis,* the eschatological Adam. The "Church of God," which is the manifestation of his universal salvific will, is thus transformed into the "Church of Christ," the prototypical element and the ultimate meaning immanent in objective redemption.

What then is the origin of the dialectical tension between "mankind" and Church? It is the historical fact of Jesus' death.

It is the breaking of the Covenant, consummated by the rejection of the crucifixion,[5] that creates the gap between mankind as an aggregate and the "Church of Christ." Although the Church is not a special community, nor a remnant, nor still less a sect, she alone is the public and genuine manifestation of mankind renewed in a post-paschal community.

The social organism of the world does not cease being a *koinonia* and a people of God, but its social structures differ from the socio-ecclesial structure of the People of God—Body of Christ, which is the institution of salvation and the sacrament of redemption in brotherhood with Christ.[6]

Obviously, at this juncture, we must establish the relationship between mankind as a universal people of God and that People of God which is the Church, the Body of the Lord, by emphasizing the fluidity of their respective boundaries, resulting from the twofold movement that draws them together. It consists in a desacralization and a (holy) secularization directed toward mankind, and, coming from mankind itself, in a movement toward "ecclesialization" through an adequate and sacramental visibility. For the present, however, it is enough to state

[3]

that, despite the above-mentioned symbiosis, the dialectical tension will be surmounted only in eschatological coincidence.

Furthermore, the Church of which we shall be speaking is not merely that sociologically situated structure which can be seen in the history of those who confess Christ and share the eucharistic table, and which is under the authority of a hierarchy in the service of Christ's love. It is also the Church as Mystical Body, a brotherhood in the making which is most meaningfully present in the love of the dispossessed and the lowly, in the apostolic ministry of the structured universal episcopate, in the awareness of every Christian, and, anonymously, in the ecclesialization process of an anonymously Christian world.

SALVATION AND CIVILIZATION

The polarization which most directly constitutes the background for the theme of our book is that of salvation-civilization, in terms of function and operation.

Both communities are already constituted *in esse,* and we shall subsequently be treating them in their differentiation and in their mutual interpenetration. The point now is to analyze their *agere.*

This analysis is all the more necessary since the conciseness of what has been said thus far might give the impression that mankind's "distance" from the Church is explained merely by the fact that it is a world weakened by sin and in rebellion against its Creator ("world" in the second sense used by St. John). Indeed, as Schillebeeckx points out, "There is, then, a distance or interval between mankind, fundamentally and historically redeemed, and the community of Jesus built upon the Rock, which is the Church or body of 'practicing Christians.' To understand this distance we must first remember the connection laid by Holy Scripture between the messianic death

[4]

—Jesus' 'going away'—and the Church, which is only post-paschal and therefore a new reality, new even in comparison with that universal reality which is the People of God. From our point of view the death of Jesus is mankind's rejection of him. . . ."[7]

However, such a conclusion would be erroneous and diametrically opposed to one of the most incisive statements of the Council. "If by the autonomy of earthly affairs we mean that created things and societies themselves enjoy their own laws and values which must be gradually deciphered, put to use, and regulated by men, then it is entirely right to demand that autonomy. Such is not merely required by modern man, but harmonizes also with the will of the Creator. For by the very circumstances of their having been created, all things are endowed with their own stability, truth, goodness, proper laws and order. Man must respect these as he isolated them by the appropriate methods of the individual sciences or arts" (*Gaudium et Spes*, no. 36).

Civilization and all that the term includes as regards social, economic, political and cultural structurization, has its own proper object and order, and the object has its own intrinsic worth.

One of the most outstanding achievements of the Council was precisely this recognition of the peculiar density and stability of earthly realities.

Historically viewed, the Council merely acknowledged the *de facto* autonomy which temporal activities had already acquired since the process of secularization began. "In this autonomy the modern world sees a summary of its demands in regard to a more or less theocratic feudalism. Both in the fields of science and politics real progress in research and social development was impossible without a gradual liberation from undue theological domination."[8]

However, it is not because the Church has become resigned to an inevitable and *de facto* evolution, that she has come to affirm unreservedly an autonomy which at times in the past she seemed to condemn, but because she has genuine respect for what is positive and of real value in the world. The Church now wishes to offer her services in order to preserve this autonomy.

". . . The Church, at once a visible assembly and a spiritual community, goes forward together with humanity and experiences the same earthly lot which the world does. She serves as a leaven and as a kind of soul for human society as it is to be renewed in Christ and transformed into God's family" (*Gaudium et Spes,* no. 40).

Obviously, then, if it is certain that dialectical tension between the Church and mankind is due to "Israel's rejection through its representative, the Sanhedrin; the Gentiles' rejection of him in the person of Pilate, and even the rejection by the hierarchy of the future in the apostles who ran away, and of Peter, who denied him,"[9] the irreducible value peculiar to civilization (even as distinct from salvation) has no reference to sin.

The Council is quite explicit: ". . . by the very circumstance of their having been created, all things are endowed with their own stability, truth, goodness, proper laws, and order . . ." and this ". . . harmonizes also with the will of the Creator."

Therefore, the Council continues, ". . . if the expression, the independence (i.e. autonomy) of temporal affairs, is taken to mean that created things do not depend on God, and that men can use them without any reference to their Creator, anyone who acknowledges God will see how false such a meaning would be" (*Gaudium et Spes,* no. 36).

Consequently, it is clear that the polarization "salvation-civilization" is not merely a reiteration of the previous one ("Church-mankind"), but a step forward. And this step not only leaves the question of its basis open, but also goes further and introduces a fresh antinomy: "autonomy-dependence."

This antinomy is of such weight that so eminent a theolo-

[6]

gian as Paul Tillich appears to reject it. Instead, he seems to
adopt a pure theonomy, in order to assure man's inner unity;
although man exists in time, he essentially tends toward transcendence. For him this is "the result of the process of salvation
known by revelation. It occurs each time and wheresoever man
as a finite being unites himself transcendentally with God, the
foundation and power of being . . . The 'situation of theonomy' is that in which the conflict between autonomy and heteronomy is overcome, because, since there is depth, there is no
need for authority to impose itself on reason from outside."[10]

Is there conflict between Protestant thinking and the
conciliar proposition on the legitimate autonomy of the temporal?

Certainly not insofar as adherence to theonomy is concerned.
The quotation from *Gaudium et Spes* (no. 36) is in terms that
reflect Paul Tillich's notion of theonomy. And there is nothing
surprising in this since it has already been made clear from the
outset that mankind and the universal "people of God" co-
incide.

We have, then, an autonomy proclaimed by the Council, an
autonomy whose legitimacy cannot be disregarded in establishing a basis for the distinction between salvation and civilization. But on what are we to base this autonomy without resort-
ing to a rejection that opposes Church and mankind?

The only possibility is to make theonomy the very basis of
autonomy as the Council does, and to situate Jesus' death
within the concrete history of salvation as St. Paul does, not
only in relation to the rejection of the crucifixion, but also
insofar as his death already exists germinally in the *kenosis*
of his incarnation.

"Have this in mind among yourselves, which you have in
Christ Jesus, who, though he was in the form of God, did not
count equality with God a thing to be grasped, but emptied
himself, taking the form of a servant,[11] being born in the like-

ness of men. And being found in human form he humbled himself and became obedient unto death, even death on a cross." (Philippians 2, 5-8.)

Although it is expressed in terms that appear outdated today, Fr. Prat's exegesis is not unworthy:

"[The Son of God] willed freely to unite with a nature subject to limitations of every sort. There are, first, the metaphysical limitations. The humanity of Christ is created and consequently finite; infinite in dignity, as being hypostatically united with a divine person, but finite in its essence and endowed with a perfection which does not exhaust all the power of God. . . . There are also the economic limitations, concerning the role and the office of Redeemer in the present plan of providence; Christ had to suffer and to die before entering into glory, and to conquer by his merit an exaltation which belonged to him by right of birth. There are also—we know not in what measure—the voluntary limitations. . . . Christ wished to be born poor; he took upon himself spontaneously our pains and our infirmities; he knew the temptations and the anguish of the agony; he made himself the slave of his adopted brethren; above all, he renounced, for his earthly existence, the divine honours which were his by right. By this voluntary self-stripping, effected in his holy humanity, the Word was stripped of himself, since he forms only one Person with that humanity.[12]

Through *kenosis,* God, the very source of theonomy, was born in poverty and weakness, not in the fullness of his glory, but limited in his power; the Son, upon assuming the human condition and sharing temporal reality, respects it, dignifies it, esteems it in itself, and keeps its consistency and scope intact. In a word, he establishes the autonomy which the Father imparts to his creation.

Let the implacable "logic" of this *kenosis* be clearly understood: *usque ad mortem, mortem autem crucis.* It is true that Jesus' death, which sets his "body," the Church, apart from the universal "people of God," is actualized solely in mankind's rejection. But it is already inescapably contained within the *kenosis* which Christ freely asumed, "being as all men are," and consequently is also the foundation of the autonomy of civilization in the fulness of its legitimacy, without its falling into an alienating dependence or being the result of some harmful negation.

We shall now relate this legitimate authority of the temporal to the Church, which as the "Body of the Lord" is the indispensable sacrament of salvation.

It is superfluous to stress that the Church is marked by the same kenotic characteristics as Christ; she is the extension of his body in post-paschal history. It is not peculiar, then, that she does not show herself to the world in the fulness of the eschatological encounter, but as a pilgrim deeply involved in the destiny of man and the world, and in their anguish and their failures (*Gaudium et Spes,* no. 1-2).

Once we have established the distinction (including the dialectical tension) between the Church as the sacrament of salvation and civilization as the work of man, we must still explain their manifold inter-relationships.

Here we come to one of the key points of this study: determining the relationships, with all their implications, between the Church in her activity in the world and the legitimate autonomy of earthly reality.

The urgency of such a task is clear when, in the practical sphere, we witness the upsurge of all kinds of confusion, deviation, mutual accusations of undue interference, or a silence that borders on complicity. Similarly, in the sphere of speculation, there is a curious vacuum: there is much talk about the relations between Church and world, both realities are mentioned as are at times their mutual conflicts; but little specification is given as to what the precise nucleus of the autonomy of the temporal is, and consequently, as to what forms the

[9]

Church's intervention may adopt, without her arrogating to herself a kind of competitiveness in the world's activity which would be harmful to the Church's own stability. In other words, we have still to elucidate more clearly the question raised by *Apostolicam Actuositatem* as to how the apparent conflict between civilization and evangelization can be overcome.

In the field of apostolic activity, this disorientation is manifested by a state of grave confusion. Many apostolic movements of evangelization tend to turn into secular movements with a Christian inspiration (or simply, into movements for social renewal). Or else, they become self-enclosed, isolated from the concrete concerns of the world, and reduced to fostering a loveless, lifeless spirituality. On the other hand, there are a great number of Christians who are committed to the task of promoting civilization and a more human development of temporal structures. Yet even they seem at times not to find fulfilment of their apostolic vocation in this activity, or else they demand of Christianity-inspired secular movements something which it is not their function to give: evangelization and witness. They act as if contributing to the "supernaturalization" of the civilizing process were not an apostolate at all.

Here we can perceive the "drama" of a Church which is *in* the world but not *of* the world. Consequently, there is question of showing that the Church is indeed present in the world, not in spite of, but precisely because of its autonomy.

There are many conceivable approaches to such a complex problem. We have, for instance, the position taken by Laurentin in his book *Development and Salvation*,[13] in which he asks whether a theology of development is possible and contrasts an Easter-oriented eschatology of discontinuity with a Teilhardian continuity eschatology. In his reply, he reconciles the opposing options by showing why development appertains to salvation.

Of primary concern to us, however, is the couplet, *Church and the political world,* and its subsequent projection in the priesthood and in politics. It is best for us, then, to discuss without further delay the polarizations which we have treated up to this point in the specific form of "Church and the Body Politic" (*Gaudium et Spes,* no. 76). However, it would be too early for us simply to tackle the exegesis of the conciliar text. We still must make a rather broad historical-notional detour, before we can fully appreciate the depth of the doctrine found in the Pastoral Constitution.

THE CHURCH AND THE BODY POLITIC

The doctrine expounded in *Gaudium et Spes* (no. 76) may appear quite enlightening today, but we must not forget that mirages are also the result of light's trickery. Paul Tillich's preoccupation with "theonomy" is a proof that a problem still exists. We have already seen that ultimate recapitulation in the innermost recesses of God is a valid concept. Yet, how can this notion be prevented from turning into a kind of "theocracy" which would be bent on "using" earthly realities merely to attain its transcendent destiny? If we respect autonomy, what reason is there for maintaining theonomy? Why insist upon its validity? On the other hand, if we support autonomy, do we not run the risk of falling into the absurd position of claiming to limit God's power? In the last resort, is not the transcendent end the only thing that ultimately counts, the *unum necessarium?*

Over the course of centuries the task of answering these questions has been an arduous one. Both within the Church and in the sphere of civil government there have been temptations to oppose, use and even absorb these notions abusively. As an illustration, we need merely recall two pages of history: medieval Christendom and the modern era, beginning with the Renaissance and the Reformation.

AN ILLUSTRATION IN RETROSPECT

The instrumentalization of the temporal

The dialectical tension between evangelization and civilization seemed to have been surmounted in medieval Christendom. Church and Imperium were co-extensive and mutually inclusive. The whole civilization process came down to evangelization: heralding the Gospel message bolstered the power of the City of God. Every human activity was "Christian" since the Church and civil society had the same homogeneous social foundation.

However, the distinctive mark of this period was not rooted in this "material" homogeneity, but, despite the formal separation of the temporal and spiritual powers, in the fact that the temporal was instrumentally subordinated to the spiritual. Indeed, the Church of Christendom *used* the world as a means for setting man on the road toward his supernatural goal. And in so doing, she suppressed what was valid in and specific to the temporal order; she deprived it of its "selfness" and reduced it to a purely subordinate or "ancillary" position (*Philosophia, ancilla Theologiae!*).

It is understandable, then, that from the point of view of the apostolate, no thought was given to the diversity of apostolic functions as is done today. The moment the role of the temporal became sacralized, the Church was able to exercise her apostolate in the temporal order only through her influence exerted *over* it.

"The ministerial function of the temporal in regard to religion was the basis for the Church's intervention in the temporal, and the Church exercised this kind of apostolate by acting in this context as a principal cause governing an instrumental one. And since the Church's action is directed towards bringing man to his supernatural goal, her governance over the instrumental causes intrinsically remained an apostolic action. In the service of the principal cause and its religious goals, temporal activities assumed a directly apostolic role. Since they were raised to the dignity of servants of the supernatural goal, their formal task was to lead men to this goal."[14]

If salvation were all that mattered, it is easy to assume that the pope alone had supreme power insofar as he was the legitimate representative of this transcendent finality. The Church was the institution through which this goal was attained, and it towered over all other orders of society, keeping them on a subordinate level.

The clearest statement of this notion was in the Bull *Unam Sanctam* of Boniface VIII, in which he pictures the temporal and spiritual powers as two swords, both under the control of the Church.

"Both swords, then, are in the power of the Church: the spiritual and the temporal. The first is wielded by the Church, the second on the Church's behalf. One is wielded by the hand of the priest, the other by the King or his soldiers, although at the bidding and with the consent of the priest. But sword must be subordinated to sword, and the temporal authority to the spiritual."

In other words Christendom did away with the antinomy between the temporal and the spiritual by means of the category of "utilization." The temporal remained subordinate to the spiritual, having the merely "ancillary" character of a tool.

Radical emancipation of the temporal

The period that opens with the Renaissance and the Reformation, from the viewpoint of this analysis, is characterized by a transition away from "Christendom" to a secular civilization. This process witnessed a progressive loss of homogeneity within the "Christian people" but also a tremendous advance in civilization; and it produced a growing awareness of the inalienable autonomy of properly human activities in the philosophical, scientific, technical, artistic, economic and political spheres.

[13]

Undoubtedly this process involved new risks, and in many cases it in fact did succumb to these dangers. The dissociation between the world and the Church became increasingly more pronounced. Freed from ecclesiastical domination, temporal values were transformed into absolutes. And this emancipation turned into a reaction that was hostile to the Church: progress was made not only without the Church, but even in opposition to her.

No one today would deny the positive aspect of this evolution, which gave maturity to temporal values and human freedom, and essential legitimacy to the civilization process, understood as the *sui juris* structurization of the temporal.

But neither would anyone deny the resulting historical error ("secularism," and the supposedly inevitable opposition between science and faith). It was and still is rooted in the desire to make the civilizing process an absolute, and in the refusal to acknowledge any transcendence beyond earthly values. In other words, it is based on the endeavor to build a humanism that would circumscribe man but also terminate with him.

Such a notion eliminates the antimony we have pointed out, but it does so not through "utilization" but through the pure suppression of one of the two poles: the supernatural.

THE PRESENT PERSPECTIVE
OF THE COUNCIL

Between the danger of asserting one reality or asserting both while denying validity and autonomy to one of them, we must find a point where the contradiction between these formulations is dispelled. We may achieve our goal by an in-depth exploration of man's teleological existence, which is the basic fabric to be discovered beneath the surface of *Gaudium et Spes* (no. 76).

Man responds to a unique salvific plan of God, who calls him to share in his divine life in Christ. However, this supernatural end, which is the sole end in which man's being can attain fulfilment, is announced and communicated to him in time. The transcendent end is made immanent in the world in the form of an anticipated participation, and, by that very fact, it is related to the intermediate ends which are situated in time and space and which determine a particular form of civilization. The world's values are not mere tools in the hand of God, channeling man to his eternal destiny. They are finalities in themselves.

With full responsibility, man investigates and experiments in every direction, creating a culture and a civilization, and thereby broadening the varied scope of mankind.

"By acquiring more initiative to the extent he exercises it, man matures as a man and develops his freedom. On the other hand, the thrust of religion calls upon this freedom to expand in its own sphere. Steps taken in time, the earth's guideposts, have their own value and relative stability, but they must ultimately open out to the supreme and transcendent step which the Lord asks man to take. Holding his hand, he helps him along the way, guides and supports him as he climbs the mountain to reach the close relationship promised him and which he will be given in the beyond, in the mystery of faith."[15]

This is the Magna Charta of the age of John XXIII and Vatican II.

For greater clarity, and to facilitate a thorough understanding of the conciliar text, we shall now explain the terms used.

Man has been said to be a teleological being. He is drawn toward an ultimate divine end and tends essentially toward it out of the highest aspiration of his existence. This tendency toward a reality which alone can fully satisfy him is to be found concretely in his life and is ingrained in the fabric of his daily occupations. Even in time, man in some way germinally anticipates the attainment and possession of his definitive object.

Everything related to the structuring of the temporal world, everything that refers to the earthly "landmarks" of man's achievement, constitutes an incipient participation in the transcendental end. It is directed from within and is intrinsically related to the definitive possession of a supernatural destiny. This destiny is, of course, reached only as an ultimate goal; but as regards intention, it is sought first, and it is definitively the only thing that gives full meaning to man's concrete existence.

For a better grasp of this point, it will be well to recall in passing the differences between an intermediate end and a simple means.

Generically, a means is anything encountered on a person's way towards his attainment of full realization, and which, furthermore, makes his advancement possible. In his striving for a particular goal, a man finds that various factors comply with the requisites of this generic definition. However, he discovers essential differences among them. One kind of means is that which, although necessary for attaining the end sought, remains extraneous to it and extrinsic to its substance. In this case, we are dealing with a simple means (a tool). There is another kind, however, which constitutes progress toward the end sought. It enters into teleological development, is intrinsic to it and ends up by integrating the finality. This means is properly called an intermediate end, because of its governing characteristic of inchoate participation in that which is ultimately sought.

In other words, the means does not become integrated with the particular end in view, but instead, it disappears once the goal is attained, since its usefulness has run its course. On the other hand, an intermediate end, precisely as an intermediary, is and must be open to an ulterior finality. But as an end, it has validity in its own "selfness," since, even though it does not attain the ultimate finality pursued, it still constitutes a kind of advance participation in that finality, and continues to subsist on its own even when the particular end in view is achieved.

[16]

Let us apply these notions to the basic polarization we are discussing: civilization and salvation.

The Church does not "use" the temporal order for attaining the eternal (although this does not mean that civilization is alien to the work of salvation). The intermediate ends are bound up with the ultimate end. Consequently, as long as a given human activity is not self-enclosed, and as long as it is "sound" and not side-tracked from its inclination towards transcendence, it is religious. Hence, we may well say that any genuine scientific or technological progress contributes greatly towards obtaining the ultimate end, which is already present within the advancement of civilization itself. The greater the objectivity we achieve in science, the more we advance in the understanding of God's own truth. When science is authentic and faithful to its own end, its objectivity is transformed into a holy reality; this secular activity acquires an eminent dignity within its own "selfness," through its participation in the divine truth.

However, we should keep in mind that this holiness does not imply a consecration or sacralization of temporal values, but rather an opening out to an eternal dimension, all the while maintaining those values within the sphere of their own autonomous authenticity.

"In becoming holy, the secular continues to be secular; changed into the sacred, it ceases to be so."[16]

This anticipation of the divine, occurring in the human, could give rise to an illusion: belief that the gratuitousness of the supernatural is destroyed and that within the temporal order itself there is an eternal exigency. Such a conclusion could carry some weight if we were merely dealing with logical categories. Historically, however, man's nature appears only as a "supernature." God himself willingly entered into history, making himself part of it; and in the incarnation, once again, we find the apparent contradiction overcome. The fact of the incarnation does not merely have a kenotic dimension which provides the basis for a respect for the temporal order. In itself it has the positive aspect of a sign that God is making himself present to man, that the divine and the human are joined in Christ and that in him the finite being is made to participate in a progressive movement which is the definitive possession of the Father. Hence, since the transcendence of the divine Person has become immanent in time, every forward step in the order of intermediate ends is a step closer to the ultimate end. Every improvement in the work of civilization is seen as an outreach into the innermost recesses of God who became incarnate in that civilization. Everything which is authentically human, and which has been assumed in the incarnation, is inchoatively situated in a new earth beneath a new heaven.

This is precisely what Edward Schillebeeckx[17] emphasizes in ecclesiological terms in pointing up the holy and even sanctifying character of the tendency towards secularization that exists in the Church of Christ. But he does not suppress the dialectical tension between this tendency and the trend towards ecclesialization which exists in mankind itself. He clarifies the dogmatic notion that creation and the imparting of grace, redemption and the building up of the Church are both conjointly treated within the majestic unity of God's Covenant with mankind. Groot[18] reaches the same conclusion in his distinction between the Church as the messianic sacrament of salvation and the Church as the sacrament of the unity of the world, as well as in the relationship he sets up between Church worship and secular culture.

"APOSTOLICAM ACTUOSITATEM"

At this point we should be able to broach a full treatment of the properly social aspects of the question, including its culmination in the political field. But before doing so, it might be useful to translate what we have said up to now into the more familiar terms of the apostolate.

"Christ's redemptive work—while of itself directed toward the salvation of men—involves also the renewal of the whole temporal order. Hence the mission of the Church is not only to bring man the message and grace of Christ, but also to penetrate and perfect the temporal sphere with the spirit of the Gospel. In fulfilling this mission of the Church, the laity, therefore, exercise their apostolate both in the Church and in the world, in the spiritual as well as in the temporal order. These realms, although distinct, are so related in God's single plan that he himself intends in Christ to appropriate the whole universe into a new creation, initially here on earth, fully on the last day" (*Apostolicam Actuositatem,* no. 5).

The way the text is worded perhaps leaves something to be desired in its counterpoint between the spiritual and temporal orders which savors a bit of dichotomy and seems to suggest a kind of dualism between the apostolate of evangelization and salvation on the one hand, and that of civilization and renewal in the temporal order on the other.

"In reality, 'penetrating and perfecting the whole temporal sphere with the spirit of the Gospel,' in certain aspects differs from 'proclaiming the message of Christ and his grace to men.' However, the first task is no less 'spiritual' than the second. Furthermore, the decree *Apostolicam Actuositatem* considered it necessary to affirm that these 'distinct' spheres are nonetheless joined together in the 'one plan of God.' In a word, the mission which the Church and faithful Christians have, in showing forth and actualizing the religious dimension of everyday life and of history itself, is not alien to the mission of salvation. It is impossible to speak solely of a super-added effect in regard to the life of the world. The word 'compenetration' has a much deeper sense, and its choice was equally as felicitous as the use of expressions such as 'leaven' and 'soul' in the passage: 'She (the Church) serves as a leaven and a kind of soul

[19]

for human society as it is to be renewed in Christ and transformed into God's family . . . That the earthly and the heavenly penetrate each other is a fact accessible to faith alone.' The Church is entirely of Christ and for Christ, her Lord. But, by the same token, she is also for the world, which finds in Christ its true meaning, its point of convergence, its center . . ."[19]

To sum up, there is but one apostolate and its varied dimensions pertain to but one reality corresponding to the one aim of Christ and of his Church. Still, the "moments" distinguished by the conciliar constitution do not lose their validity and lend themselves to greater clarification.

THE APOSTOLATE OF EVANGELIZATION

What is specific about the spiritual animation[20] informing human activity is that it is oriented towards its being raised to the supernatural, not only in the form of an incipient participation, but within the perspective of eschatological fulfilment. The function of the apostolate of evangelization, immersed as it is in the process of civilization, is religion and the consolidation of created reality with its Creator, the vivification of the cosmic in the Spirit. This activity of spiritual animation announces the salvation of every man in Christ by means of the Word, sanctifies the daily life of the Christian by communicating grace to him through the sacraments, and brings man's union with God to its fulness. The evangelization apostolate always respects the worth of the intermediate ends and stresses their aspect of "mediation," the path whereby we attain our ultimate goal. It makes use of tangible signs, like words and gestures, and even material elements such as bread or wine; but within the temporal reality it does not stop at inceptive participation in the definitive reality which it offers: man's full communication with God. This is why the Church is the sacrament of salvation, the true herald of a definitive eschatology. There is no need to stress that this fulness of recapitulation in

Christ has its culminating sacramental sign in the Eucharistic fellowship.

THE APOSTOLATE OF CIVILIZATION

Evangelization is not the Church's sole contribution to the world. What she brings to it is a Christian inspiration which directly effects properly human activities.

Critical contribution

Without prejudice to civilization's autonomy, it is the Church's responsibility to see to it that in its structure this autonomy remains open to transcendence and its gratuitousness, and thereby to contribute to man's total and genuine fulfilment. In other words, it is the Church's task to make sure that the structures of human activity are what they should be: autonomous and purposeful within their own sphere, but also receptive to the divine dimension which is connatural to the human vocation.

It is this decisive contribution which, by insuring that the intermediate ends are directed toward the ultimate end, sets deviations aright and rectifies mistakes. In compliance with this commitment, the Church condemns, as she must, unjust social orders (*Gaudium et Spes,* nos. 8, 9, 26-28, etc.), and denounces philosophical notions that deny the existence in man of anything beyond himself. In a word, she repudiates every kind of self-enclosed humanism which makes itself "impenetrable" to the values of the spirit and to God who is their souce (*Populorum Progessio,* no. 42).

The Church does not take all of these pains to defend her own interests (*Gaudium et Spes,* no. 3), but to uphold what is authentically human; and by so doing she brings a healing remedy to what is amiss. The Church knows man is a sinner and that he is tempted to set himself up as his own god. Hence, she does not look disinterestedly at a given form of structuring

[21]

the temporal world, since she is aware that some of these forms can make man's teleological progress difficult or impossible. Consequently, she reacts by denying their validity and rejecting them.

The forward movement of eschatological "recapitulation"

However, the Church does not limit herself to a contribution which in some senses is negative. As a "watcher of the horizon,"[21] she directs mankind to the polestar of its *eschaton,* its ultimate destiny. By so doing, she gathers the manifold temporal values together into a totally integral notion of human destiny.

In addition to being a builder of civilization along with all men, his brothers, the Christian aims at "man's integral development," "the conjoint development of mankind." This integralness and solidarity are possible only within a *total* anthropological notion of human existence. It is this vision that the Church offers in the light of the revelation of Christ.

"(The Church) shares the highest aspirations of men and suffers when she sees them not satisfied, desires to help them fully attain their development. This she does precisely because she proposes to them what she possesses as her own: a global vision of man and of humanity" (*Populorum Progressio,* no. 13).

There is but one possibility of the world to "be one." For man not to be merely a jumble of disjointed and misguided efforts, but rather an integral subject for integral development, he must be inspired by Christ and his Church. For mankind not to be merely a multiplicity of "peoples and nations" and a succession of generations, but rather a *katholike* in solidarity, it must have the same inspiration. Only in Christ and his Church can it constitute a totality.

In the sphere of intermediate ends, the Christian inspiration of human activity does not stress their mediation, but rather what is valuable in itself within them. By the same token, its specific concern is not religion, the strengthening of man's bond with God, although its peculiarly global vision springs from the knowledge it has and communicates of the *eschaton,* the principle of the unity of the space-time multiplicity of the cosmos. Consequently, what Christian inspiration brings to the work of civilization is not pure and simple cooperation (*opus*), but something which sets the keystone at the arch, so to speak. What goes into the work of construction (i.e. the human values of civilization) might be called "pre-ecclesial," but, because of the tendency toward ecclesialization within mankind itself, these factors can achieve architectonic unity only by and in the Church.

It is in the totalization of mankind, and not in religion, that Christian inspiration rebinds what God alone can re-unite, what he alone is mysteriously reuniting into the body of his Christ, and what he alone will definitively reunite in his Kingdom.

NOTES

1. Gérard Philips, "The Church in the Modern World," Concilium VI (New York: Paulist Press, 1965), pp. 9-11.

2. M.-D. Chenu, O.P., "Los laicos y la consecratio mundi," in Guillermo Barauna, O.F.M., *La iglesia del Vaticano II* (Barcelona, 1966), p. 1006.

3. *Gaudium et Spes. Introduction, notes et index analitique,* L'Action Populaire (Paris: Spes, 1966), note 63, p. 151.

4. Edward Schillebeeckx, O.P., "The Church and Mankind," Concilium I (Glen Rock, N.J.: Paulist Press, 1965), pp. 69-101.

5. Piet Schoonenberg, S.J., "Natuur en Zondenval," *Tydschrift voor Theologie* II (1962) 199-200.

6. Yves Congar, O.P., "The Church: The People of God," Concilium I (Glen Rock, N.J.: Paulist Press, 1965), pp. 11-37.

7. Schillebeeckx, *art. cit.,* p. 79.

8. Pierre Bigo, "Naturaleza de la presencia de la Iglesia en lo temporal," CIAS, no. 156 (Buenos Aires, 1966), p. 12.

9. Schillebeeckx, *art. cit.,* p. 79.

10. Alexander J. McKelway, *The Systematic Theology of Paul Tillich,* (New York: Dell, 1966), p. 77.

11. "Non rapinam arbitratus est esse se aequalem Deo sed exinanivit semetipsum."

12. Ferdinand Prat, *The Theology of St. Paul* (Westminster, Md.: The Newman Bookshop, 1956), 1:322.

13. Paris: Seuil, 1969, pp. 72-79 and 151-171.

14. A. Chavasse; J. Frisque; H. Denis; and R. Garnier, *Eglise et Apostolat* (Tournai: Casterman, 1961), p. 200.

15. *Ibid.,* p. 11.

16. Chenu, *art. cit.,* p. 1003.

17. Schillebeeckx, *art. cit.*

18. Jan Groot, "The Church as Sacrament of the World," Concilium XXXI (Glen Rock, N.J.: Paulist Press), pp. 51-56.

19. *Gaudium et Spes . . . Notes . . . , op. cit.,* note 70, pp. 162 ff.

20. Spiritual, that is, in the pregnant sense of the term: spiritual by the presence of the Spirit of Pentecost sent by the risen Christ to his mystical Body.

21. According to the fine expression of Roger Mehl.

II

THE CHURCH AND
SOCIO-POLITICAL
MATTERS

The advance participation in eschatological fulfilment, upon which Christian inspiration is based,[1] assumes the two aspects mentioned above: "a critical and liberating element within this social sphere and its historical process,"[2] and "a global vision of man and mankind" in which the Church claims expertise (*Populorum Progressio*).

It goes without saying that this eschatological anticipation establishes an ethic which is conceived as a discipline of the ultimate finalities (*de novissimis*) and that "from its [i.e., Christianity's] nature and from the teachings about its own special reality, certain universal norms of action are given by which man conforms himself to God, even in secular matters."[3]

This problem might be expressed in the terms used by F. Böckle. "The precise role of the Church in the formulation and preaching of concrete moral norms must be explained to the faithful. The Church's task is to preserve in her life and teaching the Spirit of Christ; the knowledgeable awareness of man's dignity and the liberating force of the Gospel. From her understanding of the faith, and constantly referring to the evidence of the scriptures, she must explain and put into practice

[27]

the commandment of love as it applies to man's life at every stage in his cultural development."[4]

The definition of this task of the Church in structuring concrete moral norms (in this instance in social and political matters) is all the more pressing since the apostolic considerations which conclude the first part of this essay might lend themselves to serious ethical misunderstanding. This indeed could happen if they were not more explicitly related to those concrete decisions to which they are bound; failing this, they would risk being accused of estheticism or even frivolousness.

In his "Ethics and Politics Today: Philosophical Foundations," W. Ölmüller warns of this danger: "If man is totally critical of existing institutions, if he cherishes a utopian hope in completely different socio-political conditions and totally unrealizable ideals, then the activities of the individual, the social group and the State will be without issue.

In short, freedom today can become operative concretely only if the individual does two things. In his activity he must recognize and acknowledge the reasonable aspects of traditional ethical, social and political institutions; and he must also create new institutions that are in accord with contemporary spiritual and socio-political problems. Neither excessive pragmatism, which does not choose to change anything, nor excessive utopianism, which seeks to change everything, will prove satisfactory. Means without ends are empty; ends without means are blind."[5]

P. Roqueplo expresses the same idea in other terms: "From the light of the Gospel, it seems to me, we can only derive the ethical demands of a given situation and these demands will always lead us to an objective and rational analysis of the means adopted. 'Evangelical deduction,' consequently, is objectively authoritative only to the extent that ethical evidence commands a form of concrete action. This seems possible to me in the case of a prophetic and 'responsive' action demanded by a flagrantly unjust situation. But I do not feel that it can be sustained in the case of the positive creation of a better social, economic or political order."[6]

For now, let us leave aside the temptation of Platonic radicalism which Ölmüller thinks is lying in wait for the anxious eschatologist. We shall also put aside that prophetic and "responsive" partiality which Roqueplo sees and denounces in the over-simplified deduction peculiar to the fundamentalist. Rather, let us focus our attention on the conditions which make both demands possible: the creation of new institutions which fit the socio-political problems of the time and the positive discovery of a better social, economic and political order.

Here we have a crucial problem of ecclesiological epistemology which we shall now examine.

FAITH AND SOCIO-POLITICAL REALITY

Karl Rahner poses the question in connection with the decisions and directives contained in a pastoral constitution like *Gaudium et Spes*. ". . . in line with the constant and clear testimony of history, such decisions and directives arise of necessity out of an encounter with a particular Church situation . . . Unless we restrict the Church's rôle to the mere proclamation of the permanent truth of the Gospel and to the indefinitely repeated accomplishment of the immutable essence of the sacraments, and unless we fail to acknowledge that it is an essential mark of her nature to act upon history in a concrete manner, we shall have to admit that her essence and her own development demand that she possess the knowledge of the situations in which she is called upon to put into action and to manifest what she is . . . This is the point at which the problem suddenly becomes awesome: how can the Church know the context of her action since this kind of knowledge obviously cannot be entirely deduced from revelation? . . . Willingly or not, she is consequently dependent upon sources and methods of knowledge which are partially beyond her control . . . We are faced with a problem to which, if I may say so, ecclesiological epistemology has not yet paid enough attention . . . How can (the Church) make obligatory pronouncements (on such matters)? In this context, how can the Church avoid the danger either of stating obvious things which are better expressed elsewhere, or else of risking statements that can be refuted by specialists in sociological analysis . . . without the Church's being able to assert in her own defence a competence which would be ultimately superior in this area?"[7]

Rahner leaves this question open. We have already made mention of his *Ideología y Cristianismo*, and even there, without any intermediate step, he jumps from "the general norms as contained in the message of Christianity and their proclamation by the magisterium within the Church" to the "open field of concrete imperatives, those special guides which shape history and the various tasks imposed by a given situation." Schillebeeckx takes up the problem, and within the framework of the relationship between evangelical inspiration and the "signs of the times," enlarges it to include the general ethical problem of the peculiar structure of ethico-historical decisions, and applies it to the problem of the theological scope of the magisterium's statements on social and political matters.[8]

It is the human responsibility of the Church to guarantee the salvation of the concrete human person. Since fundamentalism claims to draw a concrete program of political action directly out of the Gospel, it is not merely bad exegesis, but would have disastrous consequences. Such responsibility cannot be based solely upon the data of revelation; an analysis of the present condition of human society is a presupposition, since non-theological information is required.

"Political liberalism," despite the present de-politization, continues to reproach the Church for "meddling in politics" and for exceeding her own competence. But it itself is merely a false "spiritual" refuge which would divorce politics from the demands of the Christian message. What is worse, it is a kind of schizophrenia that makes theological hope irrelevant to the building up of the word and cuts away the *eschaton* of a better future upon the earth.

Despite the distinctness of the kingdom of God and the humanization of the world, both processes interpenetrate because of the presence of the *eschaton* in history. The commandment of love demands that the charity which contributes to human welfare and to the building of a more just concrete socio-political order, serve as a Christian commitment guaranteeing an authentic evangelical inspiration in the world.

Yet, what is the origin of those non-theological elements which permit the transition from the message of the Gospel to concrete political decisions?

Phrased in such terms, the problem is much broader than the issue as presented by Rahner. The Church is in dialogue with the world. To her encounter with it she brings the "data of revelation," while the world itself supplies the non-theological elements. This dialogue is not only required so that the Church can assure the contemporariness of the authoritative proclamation of her exclusive message through the conceptual (instrumental) objectivization of revealed truth. It is also most specifically necessary in order for her, in serving the salvation of mankind, to offer guidelines in this particular sphere.

It is of little importance at this juncture that Schillebeeckx extends the problem to an unverified mathematical limit. Indeed, he grants that a combination of the Gospel message and a scientifically conducted analysis of present-day society could lead to a concrete action program. But he goes on to say that this kind of analysis leaves the way open for many possible choices among the manifold concrete measures that could be taken, and none of these imposes itself as morally binding here and now. In his opinion the problem is urgent because the pontifical and conciliar documents "normally opt for a determinate concrete solution." No matter what may result from the optional illusion of reading no. 14 of *Humanae Vitae* into all the social encyclical and *Gaudium et Spes,* the problem still remains even apart from this surprising hypothesis.

Nor is it of major importance whether or not we agree with Schillebeeckx in his approach to general ethics. He opposes the dualism that holds to two sources of morality (abstract, theoretical norms which are always valid, and strictly situational concrete norms), arguing that they are incapable of arriving at a single concrete answer (here and now) that would be morally compelling (required in many cases). In addition, he feels that there is no possibility of deductive application, but only the illusion that the vacuum can be filled by some supernatural or simply irrational factor, like intuition. For him there is but one source of abstract and generally valid norms, although they are not valid as such or in themselves, but rather because they are rooted in the total experience of the historical reality of the worth of the human person. These norms are "moments," and their sole value is one of internal reference to the reality experienced. Consequently, they are merely inadequate but real pointers for the one real and concrete ethical norm: the concrete human person living historically in a given concrete society. This view rejects not only a purely abstract morality but also a simple situational ethic. Yet, if these pointers, insofar as they are genuine, prohibit the adoption of a concrete decision that is on the fringe of the direction indicated by inadequate abstract norms, they cannot lead us to what must be done here and now. The original problems still remains without any definitive solution (in the strict etymological sense of the word).

What is the solution then?

According to *Gaudium et Spes,* it is the close examination and interpretation of the signs of the times in the light of the Gospel (no. 4) and of human experience (no. 46).

Schillebeeckx does not seem to think the notion "signs of the times" worth mentioning.[9] The focal point of the statement is in the expression "human experience."

This concrete life experience, a genuine *Fremdprophetie* (external prophecy), from which these new situational ethical imperatives flow, is basically an experience of contrast. It is negative insofar as there is an absence of "what ought to be," and positive in that it is an acquisition—albeit veiled and inarticulate—of values and of a diffuse but real perception of "what has to be done here and now." Further, it is the conscience's incentive urging it to protest against society's evils and to work for its reform.

It is clear, in this view, that the concrete decision is not a "moral case," but rather the discovery of the moral imperative in its inner, immediate and concrete sense. Correlatively, the abstract norms of general validity, which are the result of later theoretical reflection (critical examination, rationalization, official formulation), are merely the projection of a long history of experience.

The transposition of what has been said into specifically Christian terms is relatively obvious. As the partially obscured beginning of the *eschaton,* the Gospel is set up as a "utopia," which results in a constant critical attitude towards the established order. Consequently, it demands a reform rooted in hope, and thereby transforms what is humanly possible into a conviction that a better world can be brought about. In other words, the Gospel is a protest, a hopeful promise and an historical initiative.

In summary, there is an experience of contrast, flowing from the Gospel, which is pre-reflective and primarily negative. From a "utopian" demand, it leads to prophetic protest, the moral demand for change, and undefined indications of a moral order. Due to a combination of theology and reflective scientific analysis, it results in a responsible and more concrete (*sic!*) plan of social and political action.

Ecclesiological transposition is equally easy. The Church, as

[33]

the institutionalized *sacramentum mundi* and *sacramentum historiae,* is called upon to make collective historical decisions because of her twofold "utopian" and "critical" function, the former being the norm for the latter. The world and history, in turn, are the expression and the translation of mankind's vocation here and now. They are the means in and through which conscience becomes explicit, as well as the responsive sphere for the interpretation of faith. The Christian's specific rôle in all of this should be that of a prophet of the Christian "utopia," directed towards the totally "new." This he does in and through the radicalization of his commitment and relativization of every temporal order.

Finally, as regards the magisterium (whether pontifical or conciliar), it should be clear that for Schillebeeckx the theological value of "historical decisions," when incorporating non-theological information about a contingent secular reality, is only that of a non-doctrinal, relatively hypothetical and conditional statement (which explains its space-time relativity, and the possibility of applying principles inadequately to the analysis of the situation). Further, the binding force of these decisions presents a rather negative aspect, without denying that it participates in the positive aspect which envelops it. In addition, this binding force emanates from a situation which exists prior to any official statement. But, as to whether the magisterium guarantees that its specific directions are the only valid ones, if this is to be taken absolutely, the answer is negative. It would be affirmative only when it is asked to be a safeguard for action that is more in conformity with the given situation.

In conclusion, what is directly required is not obedience to a teaching authority, but rather a prophetic pastoral function. No great precision can be hoped for here. Rather, because of the primarily negative character of its binding force, it is the will to overcome and an inventiveness directed towards the ultimate establishment of eschatological peace.

In its main lines, Schillebeeckx' complex and coherent position undoubtedy reflects the feeling of many believers, even among the militants, as well as the opinion of many competent theologians.

For instance, J. B. Metz comes to practically the same conclusions, although from quite a different point of view. His primary concern is with broadening and correlatively demythologizing theology and he assigns to it the same critical function of conflict with and opposition to existing reality. Theology is a secondary or post-critical reflection (a critique presupposes a synthesis of theory and practice). Therefore, since it is eschatological and consequently concerned with clarifying the relations between an eschatological faith and social practice, it cannot help but be politico-critical in itself, and not a new discipline. It is the "eschatological clause" which marks theology with a stamp of situational provisionality (although it is not arbitrary), and makes it a dialectical critique. At the same time, it prescribes a critical imperative that frees one from the present moment, and its truth must be put into practice.[10]

In ecclesiological terms, the consequences follow of themselves. The Church cannot be anything else but a critical and liberating institution. The antinomy between socially indispensable institutionality and criticism is overcome by eschatological provisionality. And it is of little importance that this has only a slight historico-social basis . . . Hope still remains.

This fresh understanding of herself which the Church must acquire not only transforms her institutional attitude towards society, but also requires a renewal of language. This new form of expression is contingent and hypothetical, relying as it does on non-theological information. It can no longer be a normative proclamation of a socio-political ordering, nor less, a system of social doctrine. It can only be a word of guidance, bereft of any dogmatizing tendency or arbitrariness. But it is not stripped of all binding force, and it is capable, above all, of giving a basis for a critical thrust towards cooperation on a common front of revolutionary protest.

[35]

This is neither the place nor the time for an examination of these predominantly critical views.[11] However, when we feel so far away from the spirit of *Mater et Magistra* and *Pacem in Terris*, not to mention *Populorum Progessio* (and leaving aside *Humanae Vitae*), it does not seem out of place to inquire whether a properly Christian social ethic actually exists. *Y-a-t-il une éthique sociale chrétienne?* is the title of André Manaranche's book[12] which is the well-spring of this essay.

CHRISTIANITY AND SOCIAL ETHICS

Later we shall see whether Manaranche succeeds in giving an answer. But first of all, we shall analyze the question with him. The model for this critical section of his book[13] was taken from Paul Ricoeur.[14]

The advantage of Ricoeur's approach is that, in addition to broadening the question to include ecumenical Christianity, it is more down to earth since it not only deals with the subject formally, *a priori*, but also in its content and its *de facto* evolution. Like Schillebeeckx, he asks what kind of operation is assumed by the Christian conscience when it works out a Christian ethic, but he also attempts to ascertain what its result is worth.

To synthesize Ricoeur's position, social ethics is a coherent doctrine constructed as a bridge between preaching as such and the technical type decisions related to ordering an industrial society. This bridge has three spans:

—the first is a biblical ethic, organizing the "social teachings" taken from the prophets, the Gospels and the Epistles, and presumed to be valid for all time.

—then there is the "social doctrine of the Church," in the classic sense of the term, an amalgam of principles taken from Scripture and notions of social philosophy (which in Catholicism is more Aristotelian and with Protestantism more Kantian or Hegelian);

—and finally, the confrontation of global systems, or rather, the critique of ideologies (socialism and capitalism, collectivism and liberalism).

Ricoeur's evaluation topples the bridge, not leaving a single span standing.

—better exegesis precludes the search for universal principles in Scripture: rather, biblical criticism invites us to restore the notions to their own context, and proscribes combining them with concepts from social philosophy;

—the metaphysics supporting this philosophical-theological reasoning has become highly problematical, and its claims to universality seem daily more suspect;

—the ideologies themselves are in a state of crisis, for they offend by being dogmatic and verbose and, furthermore, society, which solves its problems in the short run, has less and less recourse to long-range ideas.

In conclusion, the project of establishing a Christian social ethic remains irrelevant. The breach between "biblical signs" and the "techniques" of regularization is deepening. We are no longer in an age of great syntheses. It is much more pertinent to *mettre en prise directe le concret biblique avec le social précis.*[15]

Manaranche does not seem to be particularly impressed by what at first sight would appear to be a pure and simple massacre.

As for the relationship between Scripture and social ethics, he thinks rightly that the problem goes far beyond mere ethics and that the real question is what meaning Scripture entrusted to the Church can have for man today. Consequently, if we wish to avoid falling from the Scylla of naive biblicism into the Charybdis of the opposite extreme (closing the book of Scripture altogether), we must face up to the reform in hermeneutics with the knowledge that the "Word of God" is still a living word for Christians today, and it is the rereading of Scripture by the Church in the Spirit of Jesus, within the context of a given period and for that period.[16]

In regard to the tools of analysis, Manaranche retains his placid calm. "Like a discussion on faith, a discussion on ethics cannot prescind from the tools of analysis and must resort to mediatory concepts. This is especially true in the area under consideration. If the Church's word is not to be cut off from man's contemplation of his own existence and become completely unintelligible, this is doubly necessary when dealing with the social question."[17] Having said this (which is essential), Manaranche readily sacrifices the expression *doctrine sociale de l'Église*[18] as a *question de vocabulaire*. Verifying the progressive erosion of Thomistic notions and the more or less coherent character of the admixture of ecclesiastical documents with heterogeneous and ill-defined notions, he sees a new trend emerging. On one side the Church wants more than anything else to spread the "light of the Gospel" (*Populorum Progressio,* no. 2), but on the other, she is analyzing situations without any monolithic conceptional apparatus.[19]

Finally, in his judgment on universal systems or ideologies, Manaranche accepts the twofold risk of their becoming so highly abstract that the sole result will be a sterile moralism, or else of their allowing themselves to be monopolized into an endorsement of a given political option. However, he correctly questions the idea of the "twilight" of ideologies (itself an anonymous ideology of more than suspect origin), while of course conceding that a world-wide ideological homogenization is evolving as a result of secularization and demythologization. Acknowledging the "ideological function" in its true scope, and realizing that men and even Christians themselves are living and struggling within differing ideological systems, the Church still does not renounce her inalienable role of passing judgment on the ideology as such. She does so precisely because she must keep alive the baptismal fellowship among the faithful who adhere to opposing ideologies by avoiding the desacralization of the evangelical project into something political.[20]

Manaranche gives an affirmative answer to the question of the existence of a Christian social ethic and develops that answer on the four levels which, according to him, stratify its structure: salvation history, the enlightenment of the Scriptures, and the enlightenment supplied by concrete situations and concrete programs.[21]

SALVATION HISTORY

Founded as she is on the revelation of the Gospel, the Church is herself the very meaning of history and its source of reality. As a fellowship, she cannot help communicating to every man the universal ethical consequences which she continually plumbs from the message of the Gospel. This message is not subject to any "double truth," since discovering God is identical with leading a meaningful life (one properly directed) within one's own concrete situation.

This history is based first of all on the *Ecce Homo* of the cross, *the* Man (ultimate meaning, horizon of reconciliation, an invitation to take seriously even the most insignificant detail), then on Christ's incarnation (the original progressive totality which overcomes all heteronomy), and finally, on trinitarian love.

This history is also situated within the trilogy of faith, hope and charity, surpassing any faith-ideology which conceives temporal freedom as prefabricated in regard to exterior transcendence, and rejecting the perversion of Christianity which dismisses history as a tragedy by postulating idolatrous models (whether of an evolving alpha or of an omega from which the present would be deduced). In this it is like politics, which is neither archeology (i.e., the reconstruction of pre-history) nor deterministic teleology (i.e., the anticipation of what will hap-

[39]

pen later in history), but rather a confrontation of contingency. For the same reason, in her teaching, the Church leaves open[22] the free field of situational imperatives and programs, and in her directives takes the risk involved in every historical decision.

Finally, this history reconciles the world community and the human person in the perspective of the resurrection, which establishes a direct correlation between efficacy and responsibility.

ENLIGHTENMENT FROM STRUCTURES

Theological enlightenment

We shall return more extensively to this topic later. For the moment it is enough to ask from theology that it really be a *logos* about God, and that it not become adulterated into a theology-opiate. Of course, it must affirm values, but it should be more concerned with revealing meanings than with sacralizing decisions. This kind of affirmation of values and revelation of meanings can indeed be most fruitful. According to Paul Ricoeur, it is precisely the non-value of the worker in Hellenic philosophy that explains the inertia of the Greeks in the field of technology, despite their theoretical insights.[23]

Ethical enlightenment

There are ethical as well as theological systems. Every genuine human decision, if it is to be enduring, must face up to the stability of reality. Until a short while ago, the danger of "political liberalism" pointed out by Schillebeeckx prevailed: amorality by omission. Today, in line with *Gaudium et Spes* (no. 36) "many of our contemporaries seem to fear lest a closer bond between human activity and religion will work against the independence of men, of societies and of the sciences": amorality by confiscation. This morality-ideology is a short-circuit between life as lived and religion, an impatient anticipation of the eschatological end. It is not only the ecclesial temptation of Wycliffe-Huss type *pneumatikoi*, but something which also affects Marxists like Kanapa and Mury, with their constant and significant references to the Book of Revelation. It is all the more insidious when presented in the form of confiscation by way of pastoral concern (confessionalism and "witness-politics"), since its adherents believe they can base morality judgments on a kind of telepathic exploitation of the "event," sparing themselves a rigorous analysis of the situation.

If we are to avoid reducing ethics to theology, we must also not claim to reduce everything to ethics (even though all things are subject to it). We would do well to avoid any extrinsicism that considers morality to be "a bothersome piece of data in a efficacity problem,"[24] but not merely to fall into the trap of *Sachgerechtigkeit* (simple conformity to reality). Critical situations are not to be suppressed in the name of pure information and the rules of the game. Only rarely is the knowledge at hand exhaustive, even in the case of economic calculations.[25] Not only are the great majority of social objectives uncertain; they are also indeterminate. In other words, solution-decisions are very few; almost all of them are option-decisions.[26] An option is not only a *con*-clusion but also a *de*-cision, a dialectic between continuity and discontinuity which constitutes the substance of every moral problem.

Having said that, we can now mention what the manifold and complex tasks of ethics are: the gathering of adequate information, understanding and correctly formulating a problem, discerning the key points in which the responsibility of decision-making agents or centers is exercised, as well as the crucial moments of the procedure to be followed, the perception of underlying motives, evaluating the nature and importance of the interests concerned, singling out basic alternatives, measuring the extreme consequences and seeking means of conciliation, examining the urgency of the decisions and the precise moment for intervention, pointing up the long and short range aspects, and finally, attacking the causes of the evil but not without immediately correcting its ill effects.

Thus the role of ethics is specified, as well as its relationship with dogma. This relationship is not found in any kind of scriptural concordance, nor does it establish any direct "line" between a decision and the Holy Spirit. It does, however, provide a genuine guideline for the kingdom. Consequently, since revelation does not supply either the key to given events nor a guarantee of correct analysis, and since God's presence does not constitute any warrant of efficacy or competitive value, there is no room for an ethical triumphalism for post-Christian non-believers to fear. Nor, with Christians, is there any place for a crisis of suspicions that could lead to a real "interpretative imperialism"[27] on the part of what has been called implicit Christianity. A man is a Christian not so that he might be different from someone else, but out of love for Christ. He is a Christian not out of ethical rivalry, but by *metanoia*. The attraction of the Gospel does not consist in its having first place in a distribution of prizes, nor does the theological hope in total reconciliation constitute a reward for virtue.

ENLIGHTENMENT FROM CRITICAL MOMENTS

We are dealing clearly and simply with a "judgment" in the purest biblical sense. Far from being an overstepping of its mission and *a fortiori* an infringement upon others' competence, it is to be found at the very heart of the ecclesial vocation. In the words of J. Guillet,[28] this diagnosis, which is at once the brilliance, objectivity and projection out into the world of the light of the Gospel, is the indispensable condition for realistic action and therefore constitutes the first moment of every apostolate, such as Christ looking at mankind in his Gospel or Paul in his epistles. A like responsibility is discharged by the popes when they touch on critical points and stress their urgency. Such was the case with Leo XIII when he denounced atomization and proletarianization, and with John XXIII and Paul VI today, when, faced with technocracy and socialization, they insist on the widest possible participation in the work of social decision centers or in the integral and joint development of mankind.

This is precisely why the ordinary magisterium goes beyond situation theology. Were this not the case, it could be reduced in thematic categories to a conscientious agglomerate of successive statements. And the Christian would become a scrupulous curator of a doctrinal museum, when obviously he can only be a believer, faithful to a living and therefore "up-to-date" Church. By this, we do not wish to belittle theological tradition itself, but rather to call to task a particular manner in which it is used.

The epistemological problem underlying these considerations on the enlightenment afforded by structures or critical moments (inspiration, in the vocabulary of this essay) has already been ventilated. Later we shall return to it in order to clarify and explain the data on which we rely and shall treat its validity and conditioning more at length.

CONCRETE SUGGESTIONS

Lastly, there is the stratum of concrete programs, such as the world fund for underdeveloped countries suggested in *Populorum Progressio*. The sole pertinent question in this regard is the feasibility of such solutions. If Manaranche should hold them to be immediate answers to human questions, the answer would rightly be quite negative. But since these proposals do not claim any value other than as examples, they achieve their purpose which is to be a most worthwhile incentive for inventive research.

DOCTRINAL MAGISTERIUM— A SPIRITUAL SUPPORT FOR AN IDEOLOGY, OR A CRITICO-SOCIAL FUNCTION?

At this level, taking inventory of research going on at the moment, under the aegis of a more critical (and more pluralistic) Church, Manaranche becomes Chaplinesque with a syncretic pirouette.[29] Instead of continuing to operate with his expert theologian's surgical knife, he suddenly takes refuge in the peaceful coexistence of the various currents that have sprung up in the Church today. The first is more ethical, more doctrinal and more rooted in the past; and it is better suited for a builder in need of norms. The second is more political, more incarnate, more committed to the present; and it is more suited to the politician who conforms his objectives to a dynamic ideology. The third is more prophetic, more eschatological and more future-oriented; and it is more suited to the prophet, especially one who is sensitive to basic injustices and the forgotten man who lives on the fringes of civilization.[30]

If we were dealing solely with a difference in emphasis, this kind of irenicism would seem touching and even defensible. But this is not so in Manaranche's case. He sounds quite unconvincing, not only because he admits a marked predilection for the third position, the critico-social prophetic function—in which he is fully within his rights as a theologian uncommitted to any given social action—but because his treatment of the two other positions is clearly discriminatory.

Since Metz and Schillebeeckx have already expounded the third position, we shall not discuss it here. But we shall refer to the first in order to point out Manaranche's partiality, and to the second in order to give it our unreserved approval.

[44]

A DOCTRINAL MAGISTERIUM

Manaranche dismisses the first viewpoint in a single page of caricature.[31] Although he does not call it "piodocism," he synthesizes it in one sentence: a body of great ethical principles, founded on the natural law and adapted to new situations. To top it off, he assigns to it a proper social program, corporativism, as a Christian socio-political order, *versus* liberalism, in defense of an objective order over and above subjective intentions. It is also against collectivism in defense of the person against society. Finally, he barely avoids labelling it a "Christion ideology by deduction."

As regards the magisterial and doctrinal aspects, which cannot be treated *per transennam,* we shall return to them later. But, in passing, it is worthwhile to note the allusion to the natural law and the charge of corporativism.

In respect to natural law, we shall, of course, not involve ourselves in the endless polemic that is raging today. I should only like to point out that, at the very moment the notion is being subjected to radical reexamination among Catholics, Protestant voices are being raised and should be taken ecumenically as a warning. One such voice is that of Pastor Roger Mehl,[32] a professor on the Protestant Theological Faculty of Strasbourg and author of a remarkable article: *Pour une éthique chrétienne.*[33] He writes: "It is also possible that . . . the Churches and the theologians and the Reformation may have to ask themselves whether the working out of a Christian social ethic does not require, at least in second instance, recourse to notions that are intermediary between the demands of Scripture and the need for action, as well as to schemas of thought, models and utopias that may arise out of what is called the natural law. And further, they will have to ask themselves whether, for example, the notion of a responsible society[34] . . . does not properly belong to the domain of natural law."

As to the charge of corporativism, such a misunderstanding

[45]

is excusable with a man-on-the-street, but from the pen of a
theologian versed in social ethics, the error is unacceptable.
"Undoubtedly, in the past the Church has often intervened on
the level of a critique of existing economic and social systems:
liberal capitalism, and even to greater extent, socialism. But,
has she ever proposed replacing them with another system, as
has sometimes been claimed? A significant instance in this
regard is found in a statement inserted at the last minute into
the text of *Quadragesimo Anno,* (some Catholics interpreted
it as referring to corporavitism, particularly as found in
the system fostered by Mussolini). This interpretation must be
rejected because the encyclical in no way sought the restoration
of any kind of corporative system, much less one in the Italian
style. We must always be on our guard against the ever present
tendency to look for 'recipes' from the statements of the magisterium. It is also necessary to remember that the Church's
intervention in economic and social matters is not reduced
to the teaching of the magisterium but extends to the entire
sphere of Christian action."[35]

Actually, our disagreement with Manaranche is more apparent than real. Basically, it is more with an ambiguity present
in the title of the work. He wrote *A Doctrinal Magisterium*
where his intention was *A Doctrinal Synthesis.* This is so
clear that the key sentence in his three-page exposition is: "It
is this proposed synthesis that events have brought into question,"[36] followed by his conclusion: ". . . it seems difficult, after
all this, to arrive at a doctrinal synthesis, even one that is
rejuvenated."[37]

This interpretation—which in fact does not seem to be a
pure *interpretatio patris*—is nevertheless transformed by him
into a quixotic attack on a wind-mill. Indeed, it is no secret
to anybody that the systematization of the "Church's social
doctrine" is only the work of private commentators. And if
they make use of a proper hermeneutics, so vaunted by Manaranche in the case of Scripture, why shatter so many lances

uselessly against men of good will who are merely searching for some kind of coherence?

SPIRITUAL SUPPORT FOR AN IDEOLOGY

The Christian ideology by deduction[38]

The Gospel does not dictate any precise position. "The danger would be to try to find a direct means of political orientation and thereby *telescope* the different analyses and complex methods which alone are capable of being effective in our modern societies. . . . So-called evangelical politics often amounts to little more than an immature exegesis of some aphorisms taken from the Gospel, coupled with certain *a priori* ones springing from the best of intentions but with the poorest of taste in regard to the social sciences. To attempt to draw from divine principles axioms that guide political action and its alternatives is often to affirm that faith is enough to guide us in politics and saves us the trouble of having to resort to human sciences. . . . Faith is an incentive and a source of courage, but it is not a program. . . . Not a thing is given to the Christian at the start, least of all a science of politics. On the contrary, the basic political relationship is transformed by Christ. Briefly, it is the constant transformation of the struggle for survival into charity. . . . There is, of course, a Christian basis for politics, but a Christian politics does not exist."[39]

Christian ideology by designation[40]

Manaranche takes the article of Houtart and Hambye by the tail and goes into a frenzy over the poverty of its conclusions.

"The task of the Christian community consists then in formulating the ideology which in certain circumstances shows that people have become aware of this demand, and in applying it in the light of the real possibilities."

What is this very crucial demand?

[47]

Since it is to be accepted that ". . . in harmony with the eschatological viewpoint, faith is defined as a transethical reality, that is, one which does not as such produce a determined system of moral norms . . . there is only . . . a *radical requirement* of justice, equality and peace in love . . ." and "the Gospel provides the *first criterion of the choices* entrusted with the implementation of the requirement: the situation of the most underprivileged."[41]

Manaranche's exasperation is more than understandable and reminds us of Marx's reaction to Proudhon's *Philosophie de la misère:* "This position is not foreign even to recent theories (such as the *Jeunesse de l'Èglise,* for example) . . . denying a 'doctrinal' content to the faith, something which we are the first to acknowledge as disputable. . . . It takes refuge in a weakening fideism which conforms to an eschatological orientation with reference to the most destitute and with a relativization of alternatives. This is too little. Besides, it is not worth the expenditure of so much effort for so little return. The same result might have been achieved with less expense."[42]

Nonetheless, Houtart and Hambye's argument is not without interest and it is worthwhile examining it in more detail, since it touches on the epistemological-ecclesiological problem which has still to be solved.

According to them, the present confusion existing between the religious and the political, the Church and the temporal power, is fundamentally due to the lack, on the level of society, of an analytical study on the status of ideology in the traditional position of Catholic theology.

In fact, they borrowed the sociological definition of ideology from Adam Schaff[43] who describes it as "a system of opinions which, based on an admitted system of values, determines the attitudes and behavior patterns of men toward the desired objectives of the development of society, the social group or the individual." This definition presents no difficulty, not even when it is applied *intra Ecclesiam,* since like any other human group the Church can be analyzed sociologically.

The problem arises in a functional analysis of this definition. The manifest function is that of "an instrument of a synthesis, adapting . . . values of reference which permit motivation of collective action" and of "the group's constant effort to explain and justify its historical situation . . . which has a provisional if indispensable form." Without any justification whatsoever, however, to this is tacked on not only the Leninist understanding[44] of correlation between the conditions of historical existence of a given society and the representations it makes of itself,[45] but also, obliquely, the underlying, peculiarly Marxist function of idealizing and camouflaging the real structure of social relations by the dominant group.

All the inconsistencies in the article come basically from the ambiguity of the word "ideology" and from the constant and surreptitious vacillation from one meaning to another, resulting in an utterly Babel-like confusion. The same authors point out the contradictory nature of the conditions for efficacy which characterize the two functions. In reality there are two distinct meanings to the word ideology here, but in spite of this they blithely follow through the development of their inconsistent argument.

They reject the radical heterogeneity existing between the religious phenomenon and ideologies and speak sarcastically of an ethereal spirituality, which is totally unmotivated because it lacks social roots. Their basis for doing this is found in the first manifestly functional meaning.

Then, they reject it also by postulating the reciprocity and the definitive and perfect transparency of social relations in a community of the pure and the saintly. In this case, they have recourse to the Marxist sense of a falsified conscience.[46]

Next, they adopt prophetic behavior as a prototype of Christian commitment in order to safeguard the distinction between the experience of faith and the ideological function, together with the specificity of Christianity. When they do so, they carefully confine themselves to the first meaning which envelops (with suitable vagueness) the whole force of the critique, of confrontation, of the manner of operation and of interpellation, as well as all eschatological relativization which may be required by the provisional and "challenging" commitment of the Christian in history.

Finally, they banish faith to the realm of the "transethical," because of its inability to mediate between ethical decisions and immediate objectives in a given social reality, without "classifications and laws" that set off those who apply them from those subjected to them. In this case, they are re-introducing the second meaning, only to return abruptly to the first when the contribution of the sciences is brought up. As is always the case with eschatological faith, this contribution is marked with imperfection, transitoriness and precariousness.

This dissection of words may seem to be a rather tiresome juggling with semantics. But we shall see later that this is not so. The most spectacular and likewise most dire ecclesiological consequences[47] flow from this so-called Christian ideology.

The sole role left for the Church is that of chaplain to a system, a copy of the "secular arm," binding on all Christians who desire to live the Gospel. As for the priest, whether he likes it or not, he is once again doomed to clericalism, *cléricalisme à la Savonarole, mais cléricalisme insupportable quandmême.* In short, this is the "confiscation of the political by a handful of impatient eschatologists."

Christian ideology by sacralization

Once all mediation between faith and politics, including deduction, is rejected, the only thing left for this ideology we have described, in order to become Christian, is purely and simply to appoint itself. What is more serious, however, is that its tenuous specification of eschatological relativization, once it is subject to the intense heat of political conflict, runs the practically inevitable risk of melting away. Relativization goes up in smoke and it is in danger of changing into a Christian ideology-by-sacralization, with its whole train of crusades, holy wars and inquisitions.

Etienne Borne[48] denounces two equally strong contradictory tendencies: "one aggressively calls for the autonomy of the temporal order and the civil liberty of the Christian; the other, in order to make the political alternative more substantial, introduces into it the totality of the Catholic absolute or of Christian sacrality." In the face of this twofold contradiction, we must attempt a reconciliation of the two tendencies. Otherwise, while purporting to de-medievalize the Church, we shall succeed merely in fitting her into a culture on the structural-functional pattern of the United States, making her into merely one more pressure group among many.

ETHICS, DOCTRINE, IDEOLOGY, POLITICS

To conclude this chapter on the "Church and social and political matters," we must still take inventory of the manifold positions explained and discussed. We must dot the i's and cross the t's of the points in dispute.

None of the authors mentioned doubt that there is a relationship between faith and the socio-political reality, between the Church and civil society. The nuances and conflicts only affect the modalities of the relationship, and they in turn more than anything else depend on the mediations which are accepted or rejected between the Gospel and socio-political decisions.

The only author who seems to reject this *status quaestionis* is Paul Ricoeur when he asks for *une mise en prise directe du concret biblique avec le social précis.* But since Ricoeur certainly does not succumb to any kind of fundamentalism, nor less, to any Christian ideology, the contradiction is merely apparent and comes down to a problem of scriptural hermeneutics and metaphysical evaluation.[49] Aside from this, exactly as in the case of Manaranche, the crucial issue—which presents no difficulty—is that of the twilight of the age of the "great syntheses."[50]

ETHICS

There is practical unanimity on ethical mediation. It is valueless to go over the sole exceptions again (Houtart-Hambye) *qui cantant extra chorum.*

Nor is there anybody who questions the validity of its serving as a universal norm or the possibility of its being made concrete in situational imperatives.

Its articulation with theology—scriptural and dogmatic—has been treated convincingly by Manaranche, an articulation which implies neither preterition nor confiscation.

There are, of course, some discrepancies in the approach to its elaboration, between Rahner and Schillebeeckx, for example. But they do not affect the basic notion they have of ethics and its norms.[51] Therefore, the problem arises only in spheres beyond the abstract norm, within the scope of concrete application which imposes its binding force even on the situational decision.

For Rahner, as we have seen, there is no mediation apart from the concrete imperatives, from particular directives. These shape the various tasks conditioned by the situation, and thereby form history itself, while the Christian is obliged to assume them in his individual and collective decision. For him this distinction between the general norm and the historical imperative goes so far as to create a dichotomy: if the Church as such should extend her responsibility to such concrete imperatives, she would fall into an ideology that would be radically incompatible with Christianity.[52]

As we have also seen, Rahner is indeeed aware that such a clear-cut dichotomy is untenable. In giving an orientation to his "reflections on the theological problem of a pastoral constitution,"[53] he writes: "Unless the Church's role be restricted to the proclamation of the enduring truth of the Gospel . . . and unless an essential mark of her nature be ignored, namely that of acting concretely upon history, we shall have to admit as a prequisite of her essence and her own development that she possesses knowledge of the situations in which she is called upon to act. . . ." Here precisely is where the ecclesiological problem of epistemology we mentioned lies.

For Rahner, the *status quaestionis* comes down to "how the Church can know the *context* of her action." This query, at least as it is posed, savors of extrinsicism. This is the answer given: "It is the Holy Spirit who enables (the Church) to choose from among the huge mass of facts and effects drawn from (a secular) analysis those crucial points that correspond with her own charismatic calling, and which guide her decisions and directives."[54] This answer, according to the incisive criticism made by Schillebeeckx,[55] creates "the impression that we invoke the Spirit on those difficult points which we cannot explain and that we try to bridge the unbridgeable distance between general Christian principles and the many-faced concrete situation by appealing to an intervening impulse from on high which would decide the definite choice from among the many possible ones."[56]

Manaranche's comments on Rahner's captious criticisms are doubtless correct. He says: "In substance, all these doubts are the result of an ingrained habit that makes us look upon the Church's mode of expression as the result of an absolute knowledge which is unconditional and which haughtily supplies mankind with transcendent information. This is a frame of mind of which we must rid ourselves . . . it is at this point that

[53]

we have need of an awareness of the material."[57] Unfortunately, although Manaranche states the need for this *conscience du matériau,* he does not analyze it. The very heart of the problem is omitted: "how does the magisterium know what should be done in practice within the present society in order to contribute as a Christian to an existence that is more in line with man's dignity for this particular mankind in this particular society? How does such a constructive ethical investigation proceed?"[58]

SOCIAL ETHICS (OR "DOCTRINE")[59]

Despite the title of his book, Manaranche practically evades the question in his cursory treatment with its "illuminist" metaphors. In the section *Le champ structuré de la liberté,* he says: "Christian revelation, dependent here on instruments of reflection and analyses that are much more rigorous than previously, projects its light on these realities (family life, political and economic life)."[60] In the following section he continues: "the Church's task has an aspect that is more immediately historical than structural enlightenment: the enlightenment of articulation."[61]

We must keep in mind that the distinction between structure and articulation is valid. However, among the four strata constituting *la structure de notre éthique sociale,*[62] the only articulation he offers is mere ordinal enumeration.

Schillebeeckx' exposition[63] certainly constitutes a head-on reply to his own question and offers some genuinely enlightening points. Nonetheless—and in spite of his coinciding with the ecclesiological conclusions of theologians of equal importance like Rahner and Metz—it seems to be fraught with lacunae and exaggerations owing to his partiality (in the etymological sense of the word).

We have already synthesized Schillebeeckx' position, and

the following pages will therefore mention its apparent weaknesses.

We shall leave aside the over-emphasis on the "experiential" which seems to be a repetition of the irrational factor he himself explicitly rejects. The epistemological disagreement may possibly be quite deep, but, whatever the case, this is not relevant to the purpose of our work.

These are Schillebeeckx' points:

1. The correlative concepts of "non-theological information," "dialogue-Church" and "non-doctrinal declarations" (which are consequently hypothetical or conditional)—they are not so much magisterial as they are "prophetic-pastoral";

2. The sequence "generally valid norms," "the moral imperatives, their internal meaning discovered from concrete life experience," "the strictly situational concrete norms," and "*hic et nunc* decisions";

3. The relationship between "pre-scientific experience" and "reflexive scientific analysis";

4. The assimilation of Gospel and "Utopia."

Dialogue-Church and declarations of the magisterium

This present work does not pretend to broach specifically the thorny problem of the Church's authoritative competence and her magisterial function. However, we must scrutinize in more detail Schillebeeckx' conclusions on "the moral binding-force of the Church's magisterium in social and political matters,"[64] in order to be able, through a revamping of the chain of reasoning, to get back to the analysis—and eventual critique—of his basic premise, "the Dialogue-Church."[65]

Of course, within "the statements of the magisterium on political, economic and cultural questions," Schillebeeckx sets up a clear-cut distinction between "the 'historical decisions' contained in these statements" and "their doctrinal basis."

The incisiveness of this distinction stands out the more clearly in as much as for him the doctrinal is exclusively what is "directly based on the data of revelation."[66] Consequently, it alone is "directly concerned with obedience to the Church's teaching authority."[67] The remainder is "non-doctrinal,"[68] while depending also "on non-theological information."[69] and is concerned solely with the Church's "pastoral prophetic function."[70]

There is no point here in contrasting this postion with the more classical thesis expounded by J. Y. Calvez and J. Perrin:[71] ". . . the social doctrine of the Church taken in its widest extent . . . binds the believer exactly as the articles of faith bind him."[72] Insofar as the authority of the documents issuing from the Church's supreme magisterium on this matter is concerned, "exercised in a solemn or extraordinary manner, or in an ordinary manner, . . . [even] in the second class, doctrine demands the assent of faith no less than in the case of solemn decisions."[73]

What concerns us now, so as not to stray further from the tortuous path we have been following since discussing our first polarity, "Church-mankind," is to shed light by way of this distinction on the background of the concept "dialogue-Church."

Epistemologically, Manaranche's "innuendo" seems to hit the nail on the head: "What is required even more than dialogue—a dialogue which would go from a 'human' to a 'divine' information, and vice versa—is an awareness of the material."[74] Since Schillebeeckx in his article does not treat dialogue at length (and defines it only *per transennam* as "an exchange . . . where contributions are made from both sides and both sides listen to each other"[75]), the observation is in no way an importunate caricature.

Further, the distinction he attempts to justify savors of

[56]

dichotomy, when, giving more careful scrutiny to the category of dialogue, we run into this distinction more fully contained in its original premise. . . . A clear case of proof by *idem per idem*.

"The Church and the magisterium can never live *exclusively* on the 'data of revelation.' The relation of the Church to the world is not simply one of a 'teaching Church' to a 'listening world,' but an exchange, a dialogue, . . . even in the authoritative proclamation of the Church's unique message. . . . In the case of a magisterial pronouncement on political matters, this dialogue character of the Church stands out because here directives are given for right conduct in *the field of the world as such. . . .*"[76]

In plain language, the sharp counterpoint which contrasts the revealed, the doctrinal and the theological with the human experiential, the non-doctrinal and the non-theological, is merely the echo of the basic counterpoint of the strictly ecclesial *versus* the "world." Instead of toning down this counterpoint, dialogue becomes an internal part of it to the point of ambiguity.

According to Schillebeeckx, dialogue always implies a contribution of non-theological information to the statements of the ecclesiastical magisterium. But, in the sphere of the prerequisite of exclusiveness proper to the proclamation of the Good News, dialogue is reduced to the use of worldly information in order to make conceptual objectivization possible. This objectivization permits the up-dating of the Gospel message—a less than appropriate use of the word "dialogue."[77] Meanwhile, in the context of the world, dialogue would really be an interchange of contributions: the pastoral-prophetic on the part of the Church[78] and the outside prophetic (*Fremdprophetie*) on the part of the world.[79] This meaning is appropriate but it is still too inadequate for overcoming the dichotomy of a simple interchange of information.

This is a most "black-and-white" intellectual contrast, and

it ends up by reducing the whole thing to a dialogue between prophets—the pastor and the foreigner. It is all the more surprising with Schillebeeckx, precisely because he is the one theologian of note to devote himself to stressing, within the framework of the "Church-mankind" polarity, the "unity of creation, redemption and growth of the Church,"[80] to the point of the "real interval separating the Church from mankind [becoming] less pronounced."[81]

If, from the ecclesiological viewpoint the contrast between "the Church and mankind cannot be equated with an opposition between Church and non-Church,"[82] why then, from the viewpoint of ecclesiological epistemology, contrast simply the revealed and the non-revealed, the doctrinal and the non-doctrinal, the theological and the non-theological, and consequently, the properly magisterial and the pastoral prophetic?

At bottom, there is no real contradiction. The antinomy arises merely from a possibly excessive difference in emphasis. There is a marked stress on "osmosis"[83] and "symbiosis" when dealing with the subjects Church and mankind in their convergence toward full and total eschatological coincidence. Then there is a purely contrapuntal stress when there is almost exclusive emphasis on the dialectical tension between both subjects' acts of cognition—the data of revelation and "non-theological information"—in their reciprocal opaqueness within the pilgrim status of progressive historical evolution.

In other words, the twofold acceptation assigned by Schillebeeckx to his own axial category of dialogue-Church is not as radically different as he presents it.

It is not certain that when the Church proclaims the Good News with "her claim to exclusiveness,"[84] her characteristic of dialogue is reduced to pure instrumentality[85] and loses all significance in the simple *"contemporary* proclamation of the *total* evangelical message."[86] This dialogue characteristic is constitutive not only of contemporary proclamation but also of the message itself in its "transitoriness." It is not of the instrumental order, but in the order of the hypostatic union of a kenotic incarnation.

The problem, then, is not only one of "ecclesiological epistemology," but also of "christological epistemology" and, in this case, it is more precisely "biblical epistemology." In Shillebeeckx' own terms, "non-theological information" constitutes a problem at the precise "moment" that God engages in conversation with man in man's own language, and not only in the post-paschal era.

For the very same reason, it is not certain either that "in the case of a magisterial pronouncement on political matters, this dialogue character of the Church stands out because here directives are given for right conduct *in the field of the world as such* . . . because of her function of service with regard to mankind's Salvation"[87] is something absolutely new.

The problem of ecclesiological epistemology, formulated at various times, turns out to be insoluble, because it is partially bady posed. A dialogue which would pass from a "human" information to a "divine" information and vice versa, would be much more appropriately labelled a twofold concomitant and a parallel monologue. Ultimately it would be no dialogue at all because it does not result in any encounter. It is only reifying extrinsicism and notional prefabrication that demand the bridging of unbridgeable chasms since they restrict ecclesial knowledge to "revealed data" and, correlatively, world knowledge to empirical historicity.

There is no question, of course, of denying the dialectical tensions that have been so frequently pointed out. Our sole intention is to keep them within the bounds of a mutual immanence which, without in any way harming the gratuitousness of grace, could provide a basis for the reciprocity of knowledge as demanded by dialogue. In this view, there still remains the fact that in the sphere of the world the Church "takes up a position with regard to the world precisely as worldly."[88] But it is also clear that this "adaptation to the world" does not mean "desacralization" and in no way presupposes a kind of "Spirit cover-up," nor even a "natural law" at least of the *deus ex machina* kind.

Later we shall examine the conditions of this adaptation to the world which make possible the dialogue which the Church carries on in social, economic, cultural and political matters.

The sequence of ethical "moments"

In the foregoing paragraphs, something incoherent has been detected in the inadequate transposition of the ontological relationship between the Church and mankind to the epistemological relationship of their mutual dialogue. But this manner of posing the problem has already been slanted due to the reification of the subjects involved, and it becomes even more distorted when the original pair "Church-mankind" is extended over the sequence of ethical moments, the abstract element being consigned to the Church and the monopoly over the concrete to mankind.[89]

It is certain that this reproach is fully deserved by Rahner's dualism.[90] However, even Schillebeeckx' much more sophisticated experientialism does not seem completely to avoid an overly "concordistic" parallelism between the dialectical tension Church-mankind and the sequential dynamic which ebbs and flows from the abstract to the concrete.[91]

There is no point here in stirring up the many foxes hidden in the bushes of so wide and complex a field (e.g., Gospel and a one-time occurrence (*Einmaligkeit*); world and a philosophical outlook (*Weltanschauung*); salvation and history; decision and situation, etc.). Besides, it would be irrelevant to attribute to such eminent theologians a purely archeological point of view in the biblical interpretation of general norms and correlatively to ascribe an insurmountable inability to confirm their historical relevance in the face of present everyday situations.

[60]

Notwithstanding, at this point it is fitting that we recall one of the mediations mentioned by Manaranche[92]—*Le champ structuré de la liberté*—which is completely absent from the sequence of ethical "moments" anaylzed by Rahner and Schillebeeckx.

Solely for emphasis, we think it worthwhile to make a comparison between some texts of Schillebeeckx and some others which are undoubtedly antithetical (J. Calvez and J. Perrin).

To quote Schillebeeckx: These statements ". . . are also dependent on a good (or not so good) analysis of the actual situation of human society . . . the sphere of historical and contingent actualities. . . . The magisterium knows, therefore, that in this field it speaks hypothetically, i.e., given that this is the situation of man and society. . . . Such texts . . . speak of a *contingent* secular reality, [and] can only have value insofar as a *condition* is realized: given this particular historical situation of society. . . . In the meantime, *this* specific pronouncement will hold *here and now* for the whole ecclesiastical community. . . ."[93]

Calvez and Perrin maintain: ". . . the natural law referred to in the Church's social teaching contains some degree of delimitation. These ascertainable contents are unchanging and universal. They are concerned with the innate characteristics of human nature and society, which are present in every historical situation and evident in every institution set up by positive law. We can gather together, from the references scattered in the papal teaching, some of the features of society which flow directly from the natural law."[94]

No matter what we might think of Calvez's natural law terminology, "immutability" which borders on the non-historical is to be corrected. It should be granted to Manaranche that [the Church's] social doctrine could not do without the most advanced developments in [economics and technology]."[95] Yet it seems difficult to deny that these universal determinants and structural characteristics exist, and that in every situation, no

[61]

matter how historical, they appear "in, throughout, and at the same time beyond" the here and now of a present contingent situation, as the presumed object of a hypothetical and conditional statement.

Of course, even the acceptance of a "structural" mediation does not automatically solve the epistemological problem we have been discussing at such length, because it brings us to pose the same question in a different way: where would the Church as such get so privileged a knowledge of such structures?[96]

Doubtless the problem has already lost much of its tiresome inflexibility when its opposing terms are clearly reconciled: the general norms contained in the Gospel message and the universally determinant structural characteristics of the social condition. At any rate, the argument between Rahner and Schillebeeckx loses practically all its polemical harshness, since Rahner is a metaphysical theologian who does not hesitate to call "transcendental experience the proper and principal 'locus' in which the reality of Christianity is situated" and Schillebeeckx, however more historico-experiential he may be, arrives at the postulate of a concrete universal which he defines as "the *total* experience of the *historical reality* of the *value* of the human person."

But the richness of structural mediation is not only *ad hominem*. It does not *re*-solve the problem as much as it *dis*-solves it. Since they are universal determinants, the structural characteristics are not appended to the evangelical message. They penetrate and constitute it. This does not mean that they suppress the unique newness of revelation,[97] but that revelation takes them up into a conceptual union as indissoluble as the hypostatic union itself in the ontological order, as we have already discussed.

It remains for us to go back over the terrain that stretches from structure to articulation, and consequently to the *hic et nunc* "historical decision," which shall be treated later. At the moment, apparently, we have rounded the stormiest cape. Here, permit me to make a confession: the correspondence between the result of my investigations and what the supreme magisterium says about itself is a great consolation[98] and joy for me.

"Over the centuries, in the light of the Gospel, (the Church) has worked out these principles (of justice and equity) as right reason demanded, (as they apply to individuals, societies and international relations)" (*Gaudium et Spes,* no. 63).

Prescientific experience and reflection analysis

Schillebeeckx synthesizes his position on the relationship between prescientific experience and scientific analysis in the following paragraph: "Because of the continuity in man's consciousness, where pre-reflexive experience, and reflexive analysis meet in a complex unity, we can roughly distinguish two phases in these contrast-experiences: first, that of the negative experience itself, where the 'utopian' urge of the Gospel provokes the prophetic protest against man's misjudgment of the possibilities of his own existence, and where the moral demand for changes and improvements develops, with the result that in a vague way some concrete moral pointers begin to stand out; secondly, the phase where the message of the Gospel matures through a combination of theology and the scientific analysis of a particular situation into a responsible and more concrete plan of social and political action. In this way the Gospel message becomes indirectly relevant in social and political matters."[99]

There is not the slightest doubt that for Schillebeeckx this distinction of phases is clearly chronological.

"Human history shows that this is not primarily a matter of finding a *theoretical* interpretation of these 'signs of the times,' because when we do that the prophetic voice of a new moral imperative is usually heard too late."[100]

"When we listen to and analyze this voice of worldly proph-

[63]

ecy, we discover that moral historical decisions and the in-
itiation of new moral imperatives and directives are in fact
not born from a confrontation between general principles and
the result of a preferably scientific analysis of the social situation, but usually (though not necessarily exclusively) from those
concrete experiences which may perhaps best be described as
'contrast-experiences' . . . This experience is of course but the
preliminary stage leading to the proper reflection of both a
scientific analysis of the situation as of a new assessment of
principles gained from experiences in the past."[101]

"This should make it obvious that a Christian's life is not
very much helped by the magisterium proposing merely 'general principles,' for social and political issues because in that
case the Church lags by definition behind the historical situation
since such principles are at the tail end of a preceding history."[102]

In itself, this position, which has many nuances, merits neither criticism nor reservation. However, since it is not well
enough fortified against possible wrong interpretations, some
complementary observations seem to be required.

As regards chronology, if it is true in the normal course of
events that prescientific intuition precedes reflective analysis,
it is no less true that every prescientific intuition, in its totality, always rests on a scientific basis, at least as transmitted
by a given cultural milieu. It is important to note that, in this
sense, chronology goes into reverse. This contention, in no way
contradicts Schillebeeckx, and, what is more, it has the advantage of warding off any temptation to set up a Christian ideology, which, as we saw, has been attacked by Abel Jeannière.
"The danger would be to try to find a quick means for guidance in politics, and to *telescope* the difficult analyses and complex methods which alone produce efficiency in our modern
societies . . . So-called Gospel politics often amounts to little
more than the immature exegesis of aphorisms taken from the
Gospel, coupled with certain *a priori* ones taken from the social
sciences with great generosity but little taste."[103]

Without major difficulty, we share Schillebeeckx' enthusiasm for the "timeliness" of pontifical statements like *Pacem in Terris* or *Populorum Progressio*. Yet, equally enthusiastically, we endorse Weydert's warning:[104] "If the Church has a role to play in economic and social matters, her intervention must satisfy the methodological demands of the social sciences.

"The Church would not be able to grasp concrete situations by simple deduction from metaphysical principles, leaving aside any endeavor at scientific analysis. She would also remain in the realm of the abstract if she gave up all strict methodology and were content merely with applying noble ideas to situations too hastily perceived.

"The normative judgment intended by the Church (or whoever acts in her name) cannot be formed without integrating the diverse elements of a decision which in turn is based on propositions about values, the definition of a social system and diverse empirical knowledge."

This stress on the necessary contribution of science to the development of a social ethic may seem somewhat inopportune. However, it need only be connected up with the initial "Church-mankind" polarity to see its relevance.

In a different context, in which J. Y. Calvez is concerned with restoring Christian personal experience to the authentic fecundity of the community sphere of the Church, he points out: "In order to know what the 'Church's social doctrine' is in the life of the Church herself, there is no need to begin with doctrine, but with something that is not yet specifically doctrinal: the attitudes and behavior patterns of Christians inspired by faith in Christ, and, consequently, in the divine destiny of all men. The believer sees himself led to treat man with absolute respect, with a personal love in conformity with the love of the Trinity. The Christian has to invent and discover —as, in fact, he does—lines of practical behavior which are in harmony with his faith . . . (In every sense), a concrete charismatic life has priority over developed doctrine. Doctrine is nur-

[65]

tured on the life and experience of Christians. There would be no social doctrine apart from this vital experience of Christians in the world."[105]

Up to this point there is absolute agreement between Schillebeeckx and Calvez. But Calvez adds: "Spontaneous individual vitalism is not enough when we are trying to live integrally as Christians. We must live according to the Spirit, given by Christ to the community of believers . . . a community capable of a discernment that is not within the reach of each person individually."[106]

With this quote, needless to say, we have no intention of making a veiled criticism of Schillebeeckx. On the contrary, we wish to connect more closely, as we have done more than once before, the Schillebeeckx of "The Magisterium and the Political World" with the Schillebeeckx of "Church and Mankind."

Obviously, Calvez's notion of the ecclesiality of doctrine is nothing new for him. However, when he speaks of science's contribution to Christian social ethics, he fails to see in it a possible facet of the ecclesialization process making all mankind a "people of God."

For what we have merely hinted at to stand out in all its pathetic relief, it is enough to quote a few lines from Raymond Aron[107] when he speaks of "that republic of the spirit, which is the natural and necessary community of the wise."

". . . Mathematicians, physicists, biologists, separated by frontiers and dispersed throughout the whole planet, are united by invisible and powerful bonds of a commonwealth of research and intellectual norms which are unformulated but obligatory. . . . My friend Cavaillés, a mathematician and philosopher, wrote a book on mathematical logic while he was being sought after by police. As a Frenchman and a soldier, he fought against the occupation. As a logician, he continued to be a disciple of Cantor, Hilbert and Husserl. Before the court, he testified his admiration for the best in German culture. It never occurred to him that collective conflicts, including those that went to the extreme of demanding the sacrifice of one's own life, could reach into the sanctuary of thought which was faithful to its vocation, faithful to the search for truth.

"When a State or a party seeks to impose on science its subjects for study . . . it is not enough then to speak of the oppression of individuals by the collectivity. It is a question of the unlawful intervention in the activity of a spiritual collectivity by a political collectivity . . ."

On the cognitional level, how can we not see in this "international republic of the spirit" something of the "Church as fellowship to be realized" so excellently described by Schillebeeckx?[108]

It is against this background that the above-mentioned observation of Manaranche is so forceful:[109] "A discourse on ethics, like a discourse on faith, cannot prescind from the tools of analysis and must resort to mediatorial concepts. This is most especially true in the field we are studying: if the word of the Church should be cut off from the meditation undertaken by mankind on its own existence, under pain of becoming totally unintelligible, this prerequisite is doubly important when dealing with the 'social question,' which has since become a 'world question' " (*Populorum Progressio*, no. 3). Consequently, today more than ever before, science is a key factor in this "meditation undertaken by mankind on its own existence."

If there is an "outside prophecy" which calls out to her from the situation of the world, and in whose voice the Church should recognize the familiar voice of the Lord,[110] it would say unhesitantly that science is pre-eminently that voice.

It is embarrassing to have to agree with Wilhelm Korff[111] that, for example, "sociology has established itself . . . above all as 'commissioned research,' precisely because of its value in practice" and that "the assistance this science could give to the formation of judgment and to planning in the Church's pastoral sphere has, for the most part, not yet been sufficiently recognized."

We trust our readers will pardon our stressing a point which may seem marginal to many, but perhaps the old reproach of obscurantism still embarrasses us (and still does not seem to be completely irrelevant). It is certain that the paradox of a Church which does not seem at all sensitive to the demands of science is a painful thing. She is faced with a humanity which, even in its more strictly scientific empirical-positive dealings, is awakening from its long lethargy of axiological asepsis to the *appel des valeurs* in which Schillebeeckx specifically detects the call which constitutes her as the "people of God."[112]

Gospel and "utopia"

It must be sincerely admitted that Schillebeeckx' findings on the resemblance between the Gospel and utopia in his "The Magisterium and the World of Politics" was somewhat disturbing.[113] This is not so much due to the use of the word itself (which was printed between inverted commas), but especially because of one of its less felicitous derivations (at least in its one-sidedness). We shall mention only some of these: its chiefly negative characteristic as a lasting and all-embracing criticism, its conviction as to the feasibility of the humanly impossible based purely on theological hope, and the radicalism of its protest combined with the vagueness of its moral directives.

Happily, these possible weaknesses were due exclusively to the provisional inconclusiveness of a thought in the state of becoming. All of them are corrected in the excellent article explicitly devoted to "utopia" by the General Secretariat of Concilium itself.[114]

The author is clearly aware of the "social and political aspects of utopia,"[115] and even more so of its vulnerability to totalitarianism.

[68]

"It is not possible to separate the social and political aspects contained in every utopia . . . from the other aspects. . . . Behind each utopia there always lies the urge toward renewal, regeneration and improvement to bring about the best possible world. . . . The social and political aspect of a utopia is marked by a negative reaction to what went before. The utopian will not adapt himself to the concrete elements of the society in which he lives; he wants to create a new order from which these elements are eliminated. . . . Instead of the existing society the utopian wants to create an ideal society where there is no room for evil and fear.

"And so the ideal social and political man is presented as a limitless sublimation of humanity. Such a man . . . identifies himself with [human] society. . . . In this sense the concept of the Church can also begin to function as a social-political utopia but is then exposed to the danger of every ideology, namely, to fall outside reality and to become an island. . . . In such a context science itself is subordinated to the utopia: one begins to plan a man who fits into this social and political utopia."

"The positive function[116] of utopia should rather be sought in a qualitative change in the way man thinks about the future.[117] Instead of an unconscious vague expectation there should appear a deliberate and conscious expectation of the future. This will influence thought, the collective image of the aim which mankind believes it is pursuing, and the decision-making of every day. In this way utopia exercises a positive influence on the building of the community. . . .

"This change in our attitude toward the future does not yet bridge the gap between utopia and practical reality. The utopia of peace does not itself create the scientific apparatus and the ethic required to organize peace. . . . If utopia is left to itself, it is difficult to prevent it from becoming a myth of the future where the irresponsible like to seek shelter. But it cannot be denied that this change in mentality has set things going in thought, in ethics and in sociology."

Much more could be said about the "significance of utopia for theology,"[118] but in regard to the uneasiness mentioned, the essential has been said: Utopia "must be constantly subjected to the criticism of theology and the practice of the faithful. Christian conviction, however, needs these utopias in order to change the face of the earth effectively, not by an outward projection of future expectations, but by building up an ethics which enables man to achieve the expectation of the future in his own person. . . .[119] The question is then not whether Christianity *has* a future but whether it *makes* one and whether Christians can find a meaning for what they build up together with others. . . ."

IDEOLOGY AND POLITICS

There has been another study published on the theme of the distinction between doctrine, ideology and politics,[120] but here we shall only give a summary of its more relevant conclusions.

In the previous section, we preferred to place the word "doctrine" between inverted commas so as not to wake sleeping dogs. However, now that it has been stripped of its exaggerated claims to "synthesis" and its intolerable olympian magisterialism, it may be opportune to rehabilitate it since it stands for something other words cannot express, even coterminous ones like "ethics," for example.

In order to bring out this specific meaning, we shall use, merely as an illustration, the distinction between special ethics and doctrine.

Special ethics, which obviously has the same characteristics as general ethics, is distinct from it only by its projection into a circumscribed field of activities, as for instance, business ethics or the various other ethical areas.

For ethics to be qualified as "social" or go on to be called "social doctrine," it must in both cases embody in its principles as scientific a knowledge as possible of the sphere of activities included in the term social.

Both special ethics and doctrine, then, presuppose the convergence of two different kinds of knowledge—ethical principles and a given field of activities—for ethics to be able to be applied in a determined field with causal knowledge. What is the difference then?

Special ethics aims at the application of an ethical norm by a subject who is actually committed to a definite field of activity *as this field factually exists* (a soldier in wartime, for instance) and no matter what the overall judgment may be in regard to the merits of the field in question (war, in the case mentioned).

Consequently, prescinding from the ethical questions of lawfulness in regard to the acts a professional is called upon to carry out in the exercise of his profession, doctrine is centered on *the structural conditioning of the field* within which the professional's action is carried out and dedicated to the restructuring ethically demanded of that very conditioning.

In business ethics, for instance, the moralist is concerned that the businessman comply with the requirements of ethics in business procedures as they develop. On the contrary (and not "on the other hand"), doctrine analyzes the business procedures themselves. Instead of taking them for granted, it projects onto them ethical demands which can result in changing them.

Needless to say, this distinction seems to be indispensable. (Doing away with it can lead to extreme confusion.) However, it does not imply any separation. Both disciplines need one another reciprocally as complements since in everything that is human there is nothing which is not at once personal and structural.

We also feel the time has come to discuss a further distinction. It was mentioned in Manaranche's synthesis, but up to now it has not received much attention: no longer the distinction between the personal and the structure, but between structure and circumstance (or situation).

Excepting for Manaranche, all the theologians mentioned pass it over. Yet is it possible that many false steps might have been avoided if it had formed part of the problem under discussion. The preventative role played by the simple category of structure could have already been shown (a role which in this context is more of an ontological one) in regard to the "dissolution" of the epistemological-ecclesiological problem treated in the foregoing pages. The structure[121]-circumstance distinction, though not as crucial, is still illuminating.

Most of the difficulties met with by theologians when treating the problem of ethical concreteness in the "historical" decision arise from the fact that they project it from the outset in the here and now, in the singularity of the situation and in the "once-ness" (*Einmaligkeit*) of the circumstance, or in the somewhat obsolete terms of scholasticism, in the ultimate determinations of time and space.

There is no point in all this to resurrect the old quarrel over the degrees of abstraction, and still less to call up the specter of situationalism, still-born, as it is, in its peculiar unity of analysis (the situation) owing to its congenital inability to isolate it in the complex and dense context of existential reality.

The only point to be stressed here is the structural, not only as transpersonal, but even as transcircumstantial (or transsituational).

In his exposition on the particular structure of decisions of an ethical or historical nature, Schillebeeckx makes repeated reference to the relationship between ethics and science. "[Some think that a] concrete political plan of action [may be derived] *directly* from the Gospel message . . . when we combine this message with a scientifically conducted analysis of our present society."[122]

"Moral historical decisions . . . [are born from] 'contrast experiences' leading to the proper reflection of both a scientific analysis of the situation as of a new assessment of principles. . . .[123]

"The message of the Gospel matures through a combination of theology and the scientific analysis of a particular situation into a responsible and more concrete plan of social and political action."[124]

For now, we shall leave aside the apparent equivalence which at first sight is held to exist between a moral-historical decision and a concrete plan of social and political action. We shall return to that later. Restating what Schillebeeckx says, we find it strange that in the pair "ethical principles-science" there does not stand out more sharply within the "science" part the marked distinction between two of its fundamental "moments": the levels of theory and diagnosis.

That Schillebeeckx should pass this over is all the more surprising since precisely in his notion of ethical elaboration this follows, in its own way, a movement quite similar to that of science. The first part of the concrete experience of life (experience of contrast) is projected by reflection on abstract norms, of general validity. And it is also displayed in the new situational ethical imperatives which lead to historical moral decisions. The second part starts out from the empirical aspect of its field, generalizes into the (at least relative) universality of its theories, and comes down to earth through his diagnoses which set up an eventual operationality.

It seems obvious that the "ethical-science" confrontation, in which it is impossible to root every ethical-historical decision, must come about on the level of corresponding moments. Here it is preferable to designate as doctrinal only the moment of confrontation between ethics in its abstract norms of general validity, and science in its theoretical or nomothetical culmination. The moment of confrontation between situational ethical imperatives and scientific diagnoses in the field would now be simply a "working out of a model" (in a sense close to that of Manaranche's "concrete alternatives").

It should not be thought that this interchange is due to an overly eager desire for noetic symmetry. On the contrary, it is demanded by the very nature of the problems before us.

From the epistemological point of view, it would be purely naïve to claim that we can learn about "total social phenomena" (such as nation, class, colonialism or centralized economy) without theoretical mediation which alone is able to structure them.[125]

From the ecclesiological point of view, the distinction between doctrine and "model" would allow us to take the bite out of many prejudices. We do not see any incompatibility between the *ecclesial katholike,* a universal magisterium, a doctrinal generality and an "official formulation."[126] But it is clear, when we come down to a much more ideographical level, that a question remains: how can we not have a more intense perception of the contingent, the hypothetical, the conditional, and not merely the relative?

When doctrine has been rehabilitated by being given a meaning that is rather more precise and at the same time quite remote from an overly punctillious up-to-date-ness, we can then forge the last link in the chain which binds together the abstract norm and the "concrete decision-in-the-concrete" (parodying the scholastic terminology which spoke of the "practico-practical"): ideology and its correlative, politics.

Although we do not reject it outright, we shall not adopt the negative sense given to the word by Rahner:[127] "By ideology, in the negative sense we intend, we mean an erroneous system that must be rejected by a true interpretation of reality. . . . This absolutizing of a partial aspect of reality, insofar as it may claim men's assent, occurs in connection with practical matters and for that reason is usually found as the basis for political action. . . ."[128]

Here we might expect a more general and positive acceptation: "a system of opinions which, based on a system of admitted values, determines the attitudes and behavior of men in regard to the desired objectives . . ."[129]

As Schaff states, it is certain that in the sense so defined the disappearance of ideology is strictly impossible. On the other hand, needless to say, in the matter of radical rejection no one is in any way disposed to return to the panideologism of Houtart and Hambye. How can we reconcile this agreement with that rejection? By situating faith and ideology in their respective proper positions.

First, let us make a clear distinction: "Faith is not an ideology, i.e., the expression of a social group with its own conditioning and concerns. Faith is a response to a call which comes from elsewhere, an act which does not express a situation but which out of obedience responds to a summons . . . it is an accepted calling and not a deduced interpretation . . . it must not be confused with the spiritual baggage of a given social, national or cultural group, and thereby be corrupted into a Christian ideology among all the other social ideologies. When faith is thus confused with the spiritual animation of a human group, it loses its savor, its universality, its risk and its promise. It is obliged to play a "concurrential" role which sets it apart from members of other groups. It replaces the kingdom with Christian civilization, the Gospel with Christian social principles, the Holy Spirit with spiritual values, and vocation with programming."[130]

Besides, the distinction is equally important from the viewpoint of ideology: "Faith warns ideologies against self idolatry, and converting themselves into 'faiths' which admit of a summons to personal obedience and a promise of eschatological transformation, instead of continuing to be a methodolgy of rational interpretation and historical transformation. When ideology yields to the temptation to become a faith, it replaces analysis with a creed, principles with a message, a project with a vocation, the impersonal nature of the method with the cult

[75]

of personality. Ideology becomes corrupt by seeking in this way to be a summons and not an explanation. It thereby represents the degradation of faith and faith becomes the personalized degradation of ideology."[131]

However, establishing the distinction is not enough. We must establish the relationship as well. To do this, ideology—and politics—must be situated as an (unavoidable) stage in the teleological-operational phase which brings the ethical norm to its ultimate concretization as a situational decision.

Once again, Schillebeeckx sketches an answer to the problem, faultlessly, although only in passing: "Some think that [it] is possible [to derive a concrete political plan of action directly from the Gospel message] when we combine this message with a scientifically conducted analysis of our present society. On the other hand, one may say that even such a scientific analysis still leaves a wide choice of alternative measures, and does not imply that only this or that political measure is ethically binding here and now. . . . Often a number of possibilities stand open which then usually give rise to different answers according to different social tendencies, organizations or even political parties."[132]

The stratum of human activity is located where ideology and politics in its functional sense develop.

Much could be said about ideology as a discipline charged with working out criteria which would allow man to choose rationally within a given axiological framework among multiple objectives and alternatives on the basis of a scale of priorities not only of importance but also of urgency. And much too could be said about politics, charged with this same rationalization in the face of equally manifold means and alternatives with regard to accomplishing the ideological objective on the basis of the same value scales, although this time complicated by considerations of feasibility and efficacy.

We must also be able to polish the arbitrary rough spots in the above-mentioned distinction between ideology and politics, by returning it to its real complexity of reciprocal causality resulting from multivalent correlatives which are to be found in the ill-defined nature of operations proper to human reality.

For our present purpose, these rudimentary statements suffice. When we relate them to introductory considerations on the "intermediateness" of the temporal, it is easy to restore their full consistency and density, described in the case of the autonomy of earthly realities. If we take literally the metaphor of the link that binds the ethical norm to the concrete decision, we could even come to the point of conceiving it as pre-ethical. Established decisions show that not everything is reducible to morality. However, the fact remains that everything is subject to morality.

From this point of view, we ought to amend the metaphor of the link; negatively, by changing it to that of a frame, and positively, by that of a vector.

Schillebeeckx implies the first: "I can never see in an abstract norm what I must do or not do here and now. . . . Because these general norms express, however inadequately, at least something real about the concrete reality, my concrete decision must never fall *outside* of the direction indicated by these norms."[133]

Weydert uses the second, in axiological terms: "The determinants of action cannot be deduced from principles. The more universal moral reflections are, the less useful they are: *Moralia sunt circa singularia* . . .

"In action, values do not intervene in the form of models or principles, but as vectors which mark out an orientation . . . in order to make them operative, it is necessary to weigh them, to establish a scale of preferences. It is not possible to resort to a predetermined hierarchy of values, but it is necessary to try every time to dig out an optimum relationship among values."[134]

The last passages are most concise. Perhaps they are best illustrated by an example, the doctrinal judgment Peuchmaurd[135] formulates on a burning contemporary issue: that of revolution. He examines it quite sympathetically, but passing from "plaintiff" revolution to "defendant" revolution, he makes the following observations:

—the Christian should shun illusions of continual change;

—reject the myth of absolute newness;

—avoid alienation in revolution;

—"take issue" with the violence to which he may be obliged to resort, and refuse to canonize it, as was done in the past with just wars;

—put reconciliation at the very core of revolution, seeking out gestures of love for the enemy, in order to proclaim that he believes in the possibility of his conversion;

—give thought to the aftermath of revolution;

—subject every revolution to eschatological judgment, and not confuse any movement with the dynamics of the kingdom of God.

This example—as any other—illustrates, and more, makes tangible the constitutive ambiguity of every human reality. Conceptually, the distinctions are rather clear-cut. In real life situations, it is much harder to respect the integrity they demand. "The Church (too) must . . . be very aware that her dogma and her ethics, since they rise out of an historical and geographical situation whose concept she utilizes, cannot (*de facto*) completely escape the ambit of a particular ideology, despite her claims to universality and impartiality."[136]

There is no reason to regard this realistic argument as disenchanted cynicism, and even less as an invitation to prudent aphasia. Rather, it is a demand for clarity, and even more a stimulus for the relentless asceticism of purging and constant pruning.

"The Church must, therefore, refuse to become an ideology, if we mean by this an historical program which has to regard itself as absolute in order to carry any historical weight."[137] This admonition of Rahner's, which is so compelling even when he is speaking only of the "ample room for imperatives and programs that are conditioned by the situations" (i.e., politics in its most generic sense as an unavoidable "moment" of all human activity), becomes obviously much more compelling when dealing with politics in its strict and current sense.

For this latter sense, we may adopt the definition worked out by Max Weber:[138] "What do we understand by politics? The concept is extraordinarily broad and comprises every kind of autonomous directive activity . . . Naturally it is not this very broad concept which will be the basis of our discussion . . . By politics, we shall understand solely the direction or the influence on the direction of a State . . . that human community which, within a given territory . . . claims (successfully) for itself the monopoly of lawful, physical authority . . .[139] When it is said that a question is political . . . what is always meant by this is that the answer to this question . . . directly depends on concerns about the distribution, conservation or transfer of power. One who is engaged in politics, aspires to power."[140]

Read over the preliminary thoughts on the Church as the body of Christ and the extension in post-paschal history of his kenotic incarnation, in order to measure with all theological faith the abysmal distance between Church and politics. This will be the specific topic of the following pages, centering on the person of the priest.

NOTES

1. Again, as noted in note 20, p. 25, sent by the final Adam.

2. Johannes B. Metz, "The Church's Social Function in the Light of a 'Political Theology,'" Concilium XXXVI (New York: Paulist Press, 1968), pp. 2-18.

3. Karl Rahner, S.J., "Christianity and Ideology," Concilium VI (New York: Paulist Press, 1965), p. 55. There are universal norms of action, "norms which in the end will bring man to a renewed openness to God's absolute, forgiving presence in all the dimensions of human existence. We ought not to confine the faith, therefore, to any particular dimension; rather we should see it as the inner law of our whole life."

4. Franz Böckle, "Moral Sermons and Urgent Moral Issues," Concilium XXXIII (New York: Paulist Press, 1968), pp. 69-70.

5. Willi Oelmüller, "Ethics and Politics Today: Philosophical Foundations," Concilium XXXVI (New York: Paulist Press, 1968), p. 45.

6. P. Roqueplo, Experience du monde, experience de Dieu (Paris: Cerf, 1968), p. 316.

7. Karl Rahner, "Over de theologische problematic van een 'Pastorale Constitutio,' in Vaticanum II, no. 2," De Kerk in de Wereld van deze tijd (Hilversum, 1967), pp. 315-338. (French: "Reflexions sur la problematique theologique d'une constitution pastorale, Gaudium et Spes," L'Eglise dans le monde de ce temps [Paris: Mame, 1967]). See also Rahner's Das Dynamische in der Kirche (Freiburg: Herder, 1958) translated as Lo dinamico en la Iglesia (Barcelona: Herder, 1963) pp. 15-45. (English edition: The Dynamic Element in the Church [New York: Herder and Herder, 1964]). This was originally published in Wort und Wahrheit 12 (1957) 325-329. And see Limitaciones de la Iglesia: Contra los triunfalistas y los derrotistas seglares (Madrid: Cristiandad, 1964), "Peligros del catolicismo actual," pp. 119-154. This was originally published in Wort und Wahrheit (April, 1964), pp. 249-262.

8. Edward Schillebeeckx, O. P., "The Magisterium and the World of Politics," Concilium XXXVI (New York: Paulist Press, 1968), pp. 19-39.

9. Quite the opposite from Pierre Lecocq ("La Structure theologique du Schema XII," *La Nouvelle Critique,* Aug.-Sep., 1966), who sees in it "an epistemological archaism because of the presumed novelty of the attitude . . . This historical adaptation (the transition from nature to history) does not greatly change the hermeneutical intent; the signs have changed place but it is always, ultimately, a theological place that accepts them. . . . The language of signs discovers a new place in man for perceiving them, but the place has but little importance, so long at it is theological; hermeneutics shows that the real meaning is only the hidden one, but that this is given us in the complex (*entrelacs*) of the sacred words or of the prudential magisterium of the Church."

10. Metz, "Church's Social Function," *art. cit.*

11. It would be of interest at this point to be able to analyze the, at least categorical, parallel found in Schillebeeckx, Metz, and Tillich, who in 1918 formed a study circle known as "Religious Socialism." *Cf.* Eberhard Rolinek, "Paul Tillich und der religiose Socialismus," *Orientierung* (Zurich), VII (April 15, 1969), 77-80. The titles of the main passages are "The prophetical element in socialism"; "Critique as liberation toward a new efficacy"; "Over-coming of utopianism."

12. Andre Manaranche, *Y-a-t-il une éthique social chrétienne?* (Paris: Seuil, 1969).

13. *Ibid.,* pp. 96-167: "Le projet lui-meme critiqué du dedans." Prescinding from external criticism, "Le bloc deja constitué vu du dehors," (pp. 85-95) for this critique—the social doctrine as "recuperation" through pastoral fear, of Jean Kamapa; the epistemological archaism already mentioned, of Pierre Lecocq; the lack of scientific radicalism in analysis, of Gilbert Mury; the lack of *aggiormamento,* of Francis Jeanson; or the inadequacy of the diagnosis of the French Politburo of the P.C.—even should all this be quite

relevant, it does not go to the root of the problem posed here.

14. Paul Ricoeur, "Let Projet d'une morale sociale," *Christianisme social,* V-VIII (Paris, n.d.) 285-295.

15. Ricoeur, however, flatly rejects the possibility that the gospel message provides us with a direct program of political and social action. *Cf.* "Tâches de éducateur politique," *Esprit* XXXIII (Paris, 1965) 78-93, especially pp. 88 ff.

16. Manaranche, *op. cit.,* p. 124.

17. *Ibid.,* p. 125.

18. Based on Jean-Yves Calvez, S.J., "Vie Economico-Sociale, Vatican II," *L'Eglise dans le monde de ce temps,* Vol. II (Paris: Cerf, 1967), pp. 515-516.

19. "Is this a departure from the social doctrine of the Church in the traditional sense? Certainly not under this aspect. However, if we consider the collection of encyclicals and discussions of prior Pontiffs, the form of the Church's social teaching seems renewed in *Populorum Progressio.* There is here a more direct commitment in the name of the Gospel. It is without explicit philosophical deductions, without the roundabout expression of pure natural law, that Paul VI, in his own words, regards religious experience equally on the concrete level of human life, i.e., on the social level." (Paul VI and Paul Ricoeur are not so far apart as would appear at first sight!) Calvez, in *Paul VI, L'Encyclique Populorum Progressio sur le développement des peuples. Introduction et commentaire par l'Action Populaire,* 2nd ed., revised and expanded (Paris: Spes, 1966), p. 23.

Manaranche, nevertheless, shrugs off the ingenuous over-facile scheme of periods presented by Philipp Herder-Dorneich in his article: "How Can the Church Provide Guidelines in Social Ethics?" Concilium XXXV (New York: Paulist Press, 1968), pp. 80-92: The first stage of development, the Classical Period: "Catholic social doctrine was presented to us as a catalogue of *hard and fast* norms, set down *a priori,* . . . rooted in the nature of things, which never changed"; the second stage, the period of the Council with *Mater et Magistra,* in which the Catholic social doctrine began to crumble, a period of "transition from comprehensive pronouncements to special directives and admonitions; . . . the sacred philosopher would now need the social scientist . . ."; the third phase, the Post-Conciliar Period, the phase of evolution and "intellectual lobbying."

20. Manaranche, *op. cit.,* pp. 150-167.

21. *Ibid.,* pp. 171-203. Here all we have is a gathering of the material mentioned, but without the requisite explanation.

22. Recall here what Rahner has said.

23. Ricoeur, "Le Projet d'une morale sociale," *art. cit.,* p. 292.

24. Eric Weil, "Politique et Morale," *Cahiers de l' I.S.E.A.,* Series M, 14 (June 14, 1962), 14.

25. Pierre Antoine, S.J., "Rationalité et liberté de la décision," *Revue de l'Action Populaire,* 167 (August, 1963), 389-408.

26. Jean Fourastié, *Essais de morale prospective. Vers une nouvelle morale* (Paris: Gautier, 1966), pp. 144-147.

27. According to Roqueplo's vivid expression, *op. cit.,* p. 198.

28. "Gaudium et Spes et le Nouveau Testament," *Projet* (September-October, 1955), 905.

29. Chilean image used to express dexterity, in reference to Charles Chaplin.

30. Manaranche, *op. cit.,* pp. 203-215.

31. *Ibid.,* p. 204.

32. Roger Mehl, *cf. Documentation Catholique,* September 4, 1966, col. 1508-1509.

33. Mehl, "Pour une éthique chrétienne," *Cahiers théologiques* (Neuchatel) 56 (1967).

34. The Protestant equivalent of "common good" and "subsidiarity" in Catholic thought.

35. Conclusions of the meeting at Frankfurt (September 4-7,

1969) of the European Section of the Society of Jesus for Social Sciences. Report edited by Weydert, pp. 3-4.

36. Manaranche, *op. cit.,* p. 205.

37. *Ibid.,* p. 208.

38. Manaranche, *op. cit.,* p. 14. Here the author seems to impute it to J. M. Paupert, *Pour une politique évangelique* (Paris: privately published, 1965). The title is obviously none too felicitous. But it is clear what Paupert rejects explicitly, namely, that the gospel message can afford a direct program of political and social action. Consequently, there is no reason for putting him in conflict with Emmanuel Mounier, "Y-a-t-il une politique chrétienne," (May 1934) in *Oeuvres,* Vol. I (Paris: Seuil, 1961), pp. 394-406.

39. Abel Jeannière, "Y-a-t-il une politique chrétienne?" *Esprit* (October 1967) 652-653.

40. Praised by Francois Houtart and Francois Hambye in "Socio-Political Implications of Vatican Council II," Concilium XXXVI (New York: Paulist Press, 1968), pp. 85-96. The expression "designation" is evidently from Manaranche, *op. cit.,* pp. 209-211.

41. Houtart and Hambye, *op. cit.,* pp. 95-96. The emphasis is by the authors.

42. Manaranche, *op. cit.,* p. 210.

43. Adam Schaff, "La definition fonctionnelle de l'ideologie et le probleme de la fin du siecle de l'ideologie," *L'Homme et la Societe,* Revue internationale de recherches et de syntheses sociologiques, 4 (April-May-June, 1967), 50.

44. The authors attribute this to Marx himself.

45. A meaning which is consistent with the stated definition. It presents no major difficulty, for at least it does not fall into pure and simple concomitance.

46. As if the sinful condition of the pilgrim Church were not enough!

47. Manaranche, *op. cit.,* p. 211.

48. Etienne Borne, "Ethiques politiques des Eglises," in *Forces religieuses et attitudes politiques* (Paris: Armand Colier, 1965), p. 11.

49. Basically there is no real contradiction between Ricoeur and Rahner, for instance "Christianity and Ideology," *art. cit.,* p. 49:
"A right approach to the pluralism in metaphysics and in philosophy in general must consist not in having blanket misgivings about them, looking upon them as mythologies, but in preserving an attitude which painstakingly examines everything, keeping itself open to new understanding and to modifications of previous understanding, modestly trying to discover the transcendental experience common to all the systems that are offered, but which also then has the courage to come to a decision, to acknowledge with calm certitude that absolute truth is being attained in an historically determined, finite, incomplete and open-ended statement. . . ." The very "biblical condition" is already internally instrumentalized and not only by metaphysical objectivization. It would be perfectly normal for it to be not even attainable to man's understanding.

50. "C'est la nuit qu'il est beau de croire a la lumiere!" Who knows whether or not there will be another dawn on the morrow? At any rate, the eclipse of syntheses and systems, even if it should turn out to be not transitory, would not affect the substance of the subjects discussed here.

51. For Rahner ("Christianity and Ideology," *art. cit.,* p. 50) general norms are deduced from metaphysics. "[This] transcendental experience which penetrates our understanding and our freedom as the unthematic ground and horizon of our everyday experiences . . . is the primary 'locus' of Christianity, without prejudice for Christianity's history or its historicity."
Schillebeeckx, as has been said, holds that these same norms derive from the total experience of the historical value of the human person.

52. "Christianity and Ideology," *art. cit.,* p. 55.

53. Rahner, *Reflections sur la problematique theologique d'une constitution pastorale, op. cit.,* pp. 21-32.

54. *Ibid.,* p. 34.

55. "Magisterium and Politics," *art. cit.,* p. 25. (Despite the courteous statement at the bottom of p. 19: "I do not intend to repeat what he has said but rather to approach the issue from another angle without implying any criticism of Rahner, it is rather a *complementary* view.")

56. "The Spirit of God does not work as a stopgap, but in and through man himself" (*Ibid.,* p. 25, an expression little considered but quite accurate of Schillebeeckx).

57. Manaranche, *op. cit.,* p. 201. (Material [*materiaux*] in the sense of matter that enters into the constitution of a work.)

58. According to Schillebeeckx' strict formulation in "Magisterium and Politics," *art. cit.,* p. 28.

59. The best explanation of the subject is still Calvez and Perrin's book: Jean-Yves Calvez, S.J., and Jacques Perrin, S.J., *The Church and Social Justice: The Social Teaching of the Popes from Leo XIII to Pius XII* (Chicago: Henry Regnery Company, 1961), especially the first three chapters: "The Church and Social Relations"; "Revelation and Natural Law"; "The Limits of the Church's Intervention." However, the treatment of the issue is now so inadequate as a result of conciliar *aggiornamento* that the work, though substantially solid, can no longer serve except as a reference.

60. Manaranche, *op. cit.,* p. 184.

61. *Ibid.,* p. 198.

62. *Ibid.,* p. 174.

63. Schillebeeckx, "Magisterium and Politics," *art. cit.*

64. *Ibid.,* pp. 36-39.

65. *Ibid.,* pp. 23-24, 29.

66. *Ibid.,* p. 19.

67. *Ibid.,* p. 38.

68. *Ibid.,* p. 37.

69. *Ibid.*

70. *Ibid.*, p. 38.

71. Calvez-Perrin, *The Church and Social Justice, op. cit.*, pp. 66-74.

72. *Ibid.*, p. 67.

73. *Ibid.*, pp. 68-69.

74. Manaranche, *op. cit.*, p. 201.

75. Schillebeeckx, "Magisterium and Politics," *art. cit.*, p. 23.

76. *Ibid.*, pp. 23-24.

77. Not only because it would be extended to cover the simple learning of a foreign language—which, at best, might be called a condition for possible dialogue—but because, above all, it would have to be made compatible with one of its most antithetical categories: instrumentalities. In passing, it may be said, I do not see how such an inappropriate meaning could affect the relationship of the "teaching Church" and "the world pupil."

78. Schillebeeckx, "Magisterium and Politics," *art. cit.*, p. 38.

79. *Ibid.*, p. 29.

80. Schillebeeckx, "Church and Mankind," *art. cit.*, p. 91.

81. *Ibid.*, p. 87.

82. *Ibid.*

83. *Ibid.*, p. 90.

84. "Magisterium and Politics," *art. cit.*, p. 23.

85. ". . . Because the world is used to express possible truths of revelation in conceptual form, as is the case with doctrinal definitions," *ibid.*, p. 24.

86. *Ibid.*, p. 23.

87. *Ibid.*, p. 24.

88. *Ibid.*

89. General norm—concrete imperative—historical decision (Rahner); universal norm—concrete imperative—*hic et nunc* decision (Schillebeeckx).

90. Rahner, "Christianity and Ideology," *art. cit.,* p. 55. ". . . Universal norms . . . contained in the Christian message and . . . proclaimed in the teaching ministry of the Church" *versus:* "ample room for imperatives and programs that are conditioned by the situations in history."

91. This is so not only because Schillebeeckx explicitly states he does not wish to express "any criticism of Rahner" ("Magisterium and Politics," *art. cit.,* p. 19, footnote), but especially since he substantially agrees with the same ecclesiological conclusions. It is to be noted that this agreement is only "substantial," for there are several differences discretely emphasized by Schillebeeckx while utilizing Rahner's terminology. "The Christian message does not provide us directly with any concrete program for political action. On the other hand, one cannot maintain that the choice of a particular social policy is an open question for Christians" ("Magisterium and Politics," *art. cit.,* p. 22).

92. Manaranche, *op. cit.,* p. 184. Manaranche only mentions it. There is reference to what has already been said, but this only concerns the unfolding of the unique commandment of love in the plurality of multiple precepts (*cf.* pp. 66-67). He again agrees with Rahner: "Le Commandement de l'amour parmi les autres commandements," *Écrits theologiques,* Vol. VII (Paris: Desclee, 1967), p. 97.

93. "Magisterium and Politics," *art. cit.,* pp. 19, 20, 36-37.

94. Calvez-Perrin, *op. cit.,* p. 43.

95. *Ibid.,* p. 58.

96. Once the dialectical tension has been established with the reciprocal immanence between structure and occasion (or situation), it is this which is the basic objection against the natural law, conceived as a source of ecclesial knowledge distinct from Revelation.

97. Since neither does it mean—in the natural law terminology —that they lose their ability to arrive at a simple rational

understanding, for, even on being taken up by Revelation, they preserve intact their full temporal autonomy. The *kenosis* of the Incarnation is to be applied to the order of knowledge.

98. In the beautiful and strong sense of the term according to the gospel tradition of Protestantism. *Cf.* Roger Mehl, *Documentation Catholique, loc. cit.*

99. "Magisterium and Politics," *op. cit.,* p. 34.

100. *Ibid.,* p. 28.

101. *Ibid.,* pp. 29-30.

102. *Ibid.,* p. 31.

103. Jeannière, *art. cit.,* pp. 652-653.

104. Conclusions of the meeting at Frankfurt, *op. cit.*

105. Seminar of Instituto Latino-Americano de Doctrina y Estudios Sociales (ILADES), on "Presencia de la Iglesia en el devenir humano" (Santiago de Chile, September 25-30, 1968), (Mimeographed notes, p. 1).

106. We now enter on another priceless subject—ecclesiality and pluralism—and have to resist the temptation to bite off more than we can chew! However, it will be enough to point out to what extremes an irrational reaction to pietistic centralization can lead.

   According to Herder-Dorneich ("Guidelines in Social Ethics," Concilium XXXV, *art. cit.,* pp. 88-89): "Natural law can no longer be regarded as universally binding when it is a question of specific, concrete issues. Catholic social doctrine must find a *new way to prove its validity.* As of now, most pronouncements have degenerated to the level of personal opinions, and such opinions of themselves cannot have binding force. They acquire this force only if we know what group stands behind them. We must broaden the pluralistic base involved in the formulation of such opinions. . . .

   "The Church can provide a *forum* in which those who hold many and varied opinions can engage in dialogue with each other. She would not point out what is to be done. Instead, she would enable all to discuss the problems together and thus work out a decision." Manaranche (*op. cit.*, p. 216) laconically comments: "Surely, it is a bit excessive to say. . . .!"

107. In Max Weber, *El político y el científico* [translation of *Politik als Beruf, Wissenschaft als Beruf*] Madrid: Alianza Editorial, (1967) Introduction, pp. 22-23.

108. "Church and Mankind," *art cit.,* pp. 95-98.

109. See above (p. 38).

110. Schillebeeckx, "Magisterium and Politics," *op. cit.,* p. 29.

111. Wilhelm Korff, "Empirical Social Study and Ethics," Concilium XXXV (New York: Paulist Press, 1968), p. 10.

112. "Chuch and Mankind," *art. cit.,* pp. 69-70. See, for example Irving L. Horowitz, ed., *The New Sociology: Essays in Social Science and Social Theory in Honor of C. Wright Mills* (New York: Oxford, 1964; in Spanish, *La nueva sociología,* Buenos Aires: Amorrorto, 1969), especially articles by Sidney W. Wilhelm, "Scientific Irresponsibility and Moral Responsibility"; Alven W. Gouldner, "The Anti-Minitaur: The Myth of an Open Sociology of Values"; Abraham Edel, "Social Science and Values: A Study of Their Interrelationships."

Here too a fascinating topic has been opened up, but once more we must confine ourselves to pointing out a seemingly characteristic Catholic reaction, as expressed by Jean Ladrière, "Quelques reflexions à propos de l'avant-project du chapitre premier du rapport final au G.S.A.," Louvain n.d. mimeographed notes. "For me the idea of a Catholic university would be that of a *community* which would propose to face this program *as such:* there is question not only of confronting faith and scientific progress, but also of making the synthesis of both in the unity of one life, of discovering how it is possible *to live the faith* in the context of a strictly rational activity and how it is possible to animate this context by the force and light of faith. There is no question, then, of working up a

Catholic doctrine, a 'reflection of Christian inspiration,' but rather of living in community the test of reason.

"I say 'test' because the adventure of reason is really a test, a trial, a dispossession of man by the *logos.*

"This adventure is ambivalent. It is found at the very core of human reason, but opens up wide horizons (*ouvre sur les abîmes*). It would be necessary to evoke the spirituality of the Fathers of the desert as they faced up to the devil. Reason is good, a work of God. But in it slithers the spirit of evil. The situation of the Christian scientist is fraught with violent spiritual tensions.

"Nevertheless, there must be courage to persevere to the end of the adventure. For this, there is no reason that we should fear promoting an ideal *'reductor,'* a conduit, as it were, one that is strictly empirical on the scientific plane. We must realize, too, that faith does not need an idealistic language, but rather one that is strictly scientific and more consonant with science. As the scientific project plumbs deeper, the spiritual tension has more depth. And so we depart from the concepts of 'doctrine' and of 'synthesis' and in their place, we put the movement toward the mystical pole of faith. Scientific materialism is in solidarity with mysticism" (p. 14).

Such a text, worthy of Pascal, of course, deserves more than a commentary in a footnote. Its abrupt and concentrated aggressiveness cannot be refuted off-hand. However, I share Ladrière's misgivings: "I think we are entering upon a period in which the scientific spirit is about to find itself seriously threatened. Speculations on the ideological bases of science already mark the beginning of the offensive" (p. 67).

We cannot help but apply to the author his own admonitions: "It could also be said that it is necessary to distrust academicians especially, for they tend to hold unrealistic and irresponsible attitudes. If they intend to say anything concerning global society (and, at least, *a pari,* the Church, it would be necessary to add), they must submit to criticism by that society and this criticism can only be very severe" (p. 15).

113. Manaranche (*op. cit.,* pp. 21, 25) shares this disquietude:

"Must we say that we assume the reader, in his very desire for efficacy, has faith in the possibility of an ethic? For in these times of dissatisfaction, in which there is such complacency about global responsibility, it is not infrequently seen that many seek refuge in a utopia alone, without having any way to articulate criticism of the present with the model envisioned for the future. As a consequence, they fall into the posture labelled 'esthetic thinking' . . . The mediation of an ethic is necessary for dominion over history . . . At any rate, it is this conviction which motivates our research . . . Besides what real assistance, without which there is no efficacy possible, can such 'unrealizable utopias' signify for people who are engaged in these conflicts? For utopias such as these not only are content to strut in the background amid a quite aleatory eschatology, but purport to be crystallized into rigorous precepts which are utterly inapplicable."

114. "Documentation Concilium" (under the aegis of the General Secretariat) "Utopia," Concilium XLI (New York: Paulist Press, 1969), pp. 149-165. Note that Schillebeeckx is the Editor of this volume of Concilium.

115. *Ibid.,* pp. 161-162.

116. *Ibid.,* pp. 162-164.

117. À propos "Documentation Concilium" (*ibid.,* p. 163), in referring to modern sciences which "have been provided with a rough outline of the scope of their investigations in a pre-scientific state," it states that "utopia is never a *logos,*" a penetrating affirmation which should give pause to Ladriere, who does not hesitate to eulogize the dispossessing of man by the *logos.*

118. *Ibid.,* pp. 164-165.

119. And in society (the omission is inexplicable).

120. Roger Vekemans, S.J., "Doctrina, Idelogía, Politica," DESAL/Troquel, *Cuadernos de Discusión* (Buenos Aires) VI (1969).

121. Here, rather, sociological.

122. "Magisterium and Politics," *art. cit.,* p. 124.

123. *Ibid.,* pp. 29-30.

124. *Ibid.,* p. 34.

125. A significant observation so much the more vital in as much as this is precisely the level on which the Church's intervention is preferably located. *Cf.* Ricoeur, "Le Projet d'une morale sociale," *art. cit.,* third part: "La confrontation des systemes globaux," and Manaranche, *op. cit.,* "Le jugement porte par l'Eglise sur les systemes globaux," p. 150.

126. Schillebeeckx' own expression, "Magisterium and Politics," *art. cit.,* p. 28.

127. "Christianity and Ideology," *art. cit.,* p. 42.

128. "From this we may appreciate the fittingness of Lauth's definition of ideology as a pseudo-scientific interpretation of reality in the service of some political, social end which in turn legitimizes the ideology," (*ibid.*).

129. Schaff, "La définition fonctionnelle de l'idéologie," *art. cit.*

130. Andre Dumas, "La Fonction idéologique" in *Eglise et Société: Une enquête oecumenique,* (Geneva: Labor et Fides, 1966), Vol. IV, "L'Individu et le groupe," pp. 45-46.

131. *Ibid.,* p. 46.

132. "Magisterium and Politics," *art. cit.,* p. 24.

133. *Ibid.,* p. 27.

134. Conclusions of the meeting at Frankfurt, *op. cit.,* p. 3.

135. M. Peuchmaurd, "Esquisse pour une théologie de la révolution," *Parole et Mission,* 39 (October, 1967), pp. 657 ff. Synthesis in Manaranche, *op. cit.,* p. 161.

136. Manaranche, *op. cit.,* p. 158.

137. Rahner, "Christianity and Ideology," *art. cit.,* p. 55.

138. Weber, *El político y el científico, op. cit.,* pp. 82-85.

139. The word *Gewalt* could perhaps be better translated by coercion or coaction.

140. In adopting this concept we do not intend to reject the other aspect of political life as a dimension of the world and of existence; that is, the positive aspect of organization of the *polis* and the structuring of the common good. Depending on the historical period treated, the accent is on the negative—the Weberian—or on the positive aspect of politics. In periods of crisis, it is the negative aspect, that of conflict, which gives tone to political action. In periods of tranquillity, the very existence of poliitcs is overlooked.

No one seems to doubt that at present we are actually living in a period of great crisis, perhaps more violent and global than ever before. As a result, the Weberian sense of the term is predominant. It is the one that prevails today and it is in confrontation with this meaning that the Church has something to say at this moment. This, of course, does not mean she has nothing to contribute in periods of tranquillity. Furthermore, a global vision such as here presented will always keep in mind both aspects, although due to historical circumstances, only one or the other is stressed.

III

PRIESTHOOD
AND POLITICS[1]

THE TERMS OF THE PROBLEM

Up to now we have been discussing the Church in her entirety, as the people of God and the Body of Christ, with only a few references to her hierarchical structure, particularly in regard to the magisterium. But there is no doubt that the "Church-politics" polarity becomes more taut when treated as a "priesthood-politics" polarity, since in the Church the priest is the protagonist of the eucharistic anamnesis and the minister consecrated to the divine Word. This is a further reason, then, for specifying more diligently the opposing terms.

As we have already said, the term "politics" is taken here in its strict sense. We are not taking it in Weber's sense when he says that "we are all politicians occasionally . . . when we vote, applaud or protest at a political meeting . . . or manifest our will in some other analogous manner,"[2] but rather in his other sense when he speaks of "professional" politics. In the life of today's priest-citizen, this could be understood as militancy in spreading a given ideology and linking up with a current definite political action (which might possibly but not necessarily be tied up with a particular party).

We shall consider the priest as a "pure type" (to use Weber's terminology), i.e., a priest exclusively dedicated to his ministry

[95]

and to the preaching of the Word within the unlimited mobility of the evangelical apostolate.[3]

The more usual way of posing the problem of the relationship between the priest and politics is to do so in terms of incompatibility. Although this is not wrong, it is unfortunate. It approaches the issue from a negative standpoint as if the priesthood could be defined starting out from an alpha privative. In this view which is all too wide-spread, the priest is only that rare man who is *not* married, practises *no* profession, and—for our particular concern—who does *not* engage in politics. ". . . Setting the priest up, externally, as the antithesis of 'man' is really distressing. For the priesthood precisely is an authentic manner of being a man: it is a service by a man for men."[4]

It is clear that we cannot ignore the negative factors underlying the dialectical tension between Church and mankind, evangelization and civilization, and consequently between the priesthood and politics. This dialectical tension, however, must be eased not by "fluidity of the boundaries,"[5] nor still less by the absence of commitment, but rather by the specifically priestly modality of commitment[6] in politics. It is not a question of choosing between a commitment to politics or a non-commitment, but between two kinds of commitment.

A fortiori, it is quite unfortunate to pose the problem, in what until recently were the classic terms of essential incompatibility. Independently from the fact that it is notional and non-historical, it sounds quite unconvincing since it tries to prove too much and by-passes the real questions.

In the definition of priesthood, there is nothing which intrinsically contradicts a temporal commitment. Set apart within the people of God, the Church of Christ and mankind, but not outside of it, on the fringes or still less above it, the priest is still a man among men, a citizen of the *earthly city.* He is one with all men and thus impelled to contribute to this solidarity in proportion to his own competence. "The priest is not a super-Christian. His priesthood is not an amplification of the term Christian. It is found in another order of things, because within the bosom of the Church it constitutes a special function or service,"[7] which, as we shall see, does not place him above civil society.

Nor, for the moment, is there anything about politics that should keep it aloof from the priesthood. Certainly it has its dangers—unbridled passions, hatreds, blind violence, moral compromises—in proportion to its responsibilities. But dangers must be confronted, not escaped.

Besides, these dangers lie in wait not only for priests, but for every layman, and we see no reason why the laity should have to "soil their hands," while the clergy remain "pure" and uncontaminated. The risks entailed in politics, as in every other human activity, do not preclude the priest's becoming involved. They call upon him to face up to them frankly so he might fend them off or at least treat them as they deserve, as consciously assumed risks without the stigma of sin so often attributed to them.

To one of his sons sent on a dangerous mission, Saint Ignatius wrote: "Even the (motive) for your safety does not seem valid to me . . . if in our vocation we seek only to walk in safety and if it were necessary to relinquish the good we should be doing in order to keep us far from any danger, it would not be worthwhile to live and deal with our neighbor. But our vocation is to deal with all men."[8]

The most harmful thing about this "essentialist" approach is that it tends to strip the priest of the integrity of his manhood and correlatively to denigrate politics as something dirty (as if to justify himself, the celibate had to belittle marriage, while he should be doing the opposite).

Consequently, there is nothing inherently unhealthy about the anguish felt by so many priests who today more than ever are asking themselves what politics may be demanding of them. Up to twenty years ago, this anguish affected only a few—remember the worker priests—who were moved to involve themselves in a mission to dechristianized milieus. Today, however, everyone is involved who lives in a world that is secularized or well on the way to becoming so. It is against this background that the questions of the day must be examined in order to do them justice.

In Latin America, the situation is infinitely more dramatic still. It is not only a world on the way to secularization, but an "intolerable" world, in the throes of a vast revolutionary drive. And priests—or at least many of them, especially the young—feel torn between dissatisfaction with Christian society—and at times with theocracy—and the pressing demands of a world in the process of being born. "Divided between the attraction of the past and the hopes they bring for the future, these new apostles have not immediately found the new style needed . . . The Church of today must evangelize the world of today and not some form of non-existent Christianity whose restoration historical evolution would render more than impossible. The apostle is not obliged to chase after a chimera."[9]

What is more natural for the priest, then, than that he become painfully aware of being *Heimatvertrieben,* a displaced person, and that he question his place in the world and society!

The priest is a man in the full sense of the word and he can rightly apply to himself the old Roman adage: *Homo sum et nihil humanum a me alienum puto.* "An apostolic life is compatible with various occupations. People have tried in vain to label certain kinds of employment as unworthy of the priest: manual labor . . . teaching . . . research . . . It is obvious that an apostle must go wherever men are."[10] Therefore, nothing human is alien, much less forbidden, to a priest. Nor does any political community, traumatized by the clericalism of the past, have any reason to ostracize one of its citizens, as if the priesthood could be a reason for restricting the exercise of a human or civil right.

Moreover, political involvement is not only a matter of a right. It can be a duty, and often is. However, due to the nature of the priesthood, it is a special kind of involvement. It is not a political involvement with the political, but a priestly involvement with the political. In what follows we shall see what this means exactly and what is the true dimension of the priest's involvement in politics.

CULTIC PRIESTHOOD AND POLITICS

The priesthood is the sign and guarantee of eucharistic unity in the Church. "The celebration of the Eucharist is the most intensive event of the Church. . . . It is not only true that the Eucharist exists because the Church exists; it is also true, if rightly understood, that the Church exists because the Eucharist exists. The Church is and remains even as a whole, only because she is actualized again and again in the one all-embracing 'event' of herself, that is, in the Eucharist."[11] The eucharistic anamnesis, then, is the re-actualization *in* the world of the salvific presence of Christ and his body the Church, and at the same time constitutes the "sacrament of supreme unity," as Rahner calls it, because it is the sign of the transcendant unity of men among themselves and of men with God. It is the offering of Christ, through the mediation of the priest, to *all* men. This is why the Eucharist is considered to be the fundamental sacrament towards which all the others tend.

"The union of all communicants in the body and blood of Christ perfects Christ's ecclesial body by uniting them with one another in Christ's humanity, and God's personal presence in this unifying humanity unites men to God and gives life to all the sons of God's family."[12]

This sacrament and efficacious principle of union is fundamental in itself and is all the more important and necessary today on account of the acknowledged tendency to pluralism, even in ethics, on the part of the Christian community, with all

[99]

its consequences that ultimately determine differing and irreconcilable political positions arising from cleavages and ruptures over political matter.

The key point of priestly life, then, is that power not of evoking but of effectively bringing the humanity of Christ and the presence of God to the concrete present through the mystery of the Eucharist uniting a plurality of men around the table of sacrifice. It is a ministry that gives the priest a special dignity and manifests his temporal and eternal nature: eternal because he unites men with the absolute transcendence, and temporal because he exercises it within a given time-space community in forms that are constantly renewed for the present moment.

What has been said does away with the figure of the priest previously defined *negatively*. On the contrary, in this light he is precisely the *positive* man, the one who is able essentially to communicate to man with God,[13] who "brings the sacrifice of Christ to a sacramental, visible presence before the celebrating community. In their presence he is not only a guiding pastor and a prophet of God's word; he is also the sacramental representative of the sacrificing Christ."[14] The priest is not on the sidelines of the community but in its midst. He is the unifier who, at a climactic moment of ontological relationship, permits the unification of solidarities that are separated by different ethical, ideological and political options. He is the mediator of the One who committed himself unto death for mankind, and insofar as he is his representative, this solidarity encompasses him . . . The priest does not say "this is the body of Christ and this is the blood of Christ," but rather "this is *my* body and this is *my* blood." Hence, in these days of "commitment" there is no need to look further for a commitment for the priest. He is essentially committed at man's very root and, by that very fact, with all that manifests his humanity, in all spheres of his life, including the political, from this point on. Nor are we to think that the Eucharist is simply a celebration, since it ". . . embraces the apostle's whole life and exerts influence over the entire world far beyond the bounds of an assembly. The whole apostolate enters into the mass, and every mass is a 'mass by and for the world.' "[15]

What happens, then, if this priest, who is the sign and seal of eucharistic unity in the Church, aligns himself with a particular current of political action and fights for its accession to power—which is the nature of every political movement—in the exercise of his ministry?

One does not have to be especially perceptive to foresee that in the first place the priest would become an element disruptive of the unity he is supposed to safeguard and would be incapable of bringing the Christian community together in the preeminent sacrament of union. "It would be blatantly unjust to seek to oblige them to alienate themselves under common political options . . . this would involve a superficial and fragile unity which, first in the spirit of the faithful and then among non-Catholics, would adulterate the very meaning of the people of God and the Church's respect for the internal diversity of political society."[16] If we accept, as Weber asserts, that the means proper to politics is violence, we should also have to accept that what in this case would unite Christians would be violence itself, even though this violence would be "legitimized": through recourse to theology. The priest's political concerns—ever urgent and absolutizing—would become so important that Christ "would become a meaningless formality in the face of the 'real problems.' "[17] The eucharistic anamnesis would thereby lose all its meaning and content and would become an irrelevant rite, bereft of all meaning. Immediately, from the moment it loses its unifying character, it also loses much of its meaning. If it is through the Eucharist that the priest becomes an apostle, as Rahner basically assures us,[18] when the Eucharist is emptied of meaning or when the meaning itself is replaced by political concerns (even though there may be sound reasons for this), it will not be hard to "guess" that such an "apostolate" (would it not perhaps be better to call it "proselytism"?), torn from its foundation, will turn into an ideology—with all the dangers pointed out above. Nor will it be hard to "guess" either that it will become the departure point for a new Crusade, imposing the Gospel by blood and fire, by force and political pressure. How contradictory this would be to the kenotic character of Christ's Church, a pilgrim, without power, in the service of the whole of mankind!

The priest's commitment to uniting men among themselves and with God would turn into militancy and his solidarity would not go beyond a solidarity of a coterie. The genuine dimensions of the commitment would become diluted and the very meaning of the priesthood itself betrayed. It would be a more modern and sophisticated version of Peter's denial which would proffer many reasons in its own favor.

Against this watered down meaning, Manaranche's words ring true: "Uniting in the Eucharist men who have quite solid reasons for being at odds, by showing them that this 'hostility' must be stripped, in Christ, of all 'enmity' (this is the difference between *hostis* and *inimicus*), is excellent pedagogy for political life. We do not see how anyone (but a priest) could do this. Devoting one's whole life to such a task amply suffices to make one's existence meaningful. Nostalgia for political action is dangerous when it arises out of a loss of meaning."[19]

It must be clearly understood that this is not separating the priest from politics so as to keep him uncontaminated by such a "problematical" worldly activity. On the contrary, it is placing him right in the center of human activity, at the critical point of an essential commitment, in which solidarity regains its full significance in an eschatological perspective of the kingdom of God. We are merely pointing out the bankruptcy which results when the priest abandons this commitment for politics and defrauds the Christian community which expects something else from him . . . The arguments about the supposed "immaturity" of such a community, which makes the priest appear "misunderstood," hold little water.

[102]

THE PRIESTHOOD OF THE
WORD AND POLITICS

The priest "will also have the mission of unifying a community which will be living, on an ever increasing scale perhaps, widely spread apart throughout the world. This he will do by proclaiming the word of God which springs from the Eucharist and leads to it: the word and the Eucharist which unite the community in the Holy Spirit, not to separate it from the world, but to give thanks to the Father for the world through Jesus Christ, and also to signify and bring about in this mystery ised through the resurrection and the second coming of the the fulfilment to which the world tends and which God prom-Lord."[20]

The word is also the instrument of union among Christians, and is nurtured by the Eucharist. Hence a Eucharist which has lost its meaning will be sorely unfit to nourish and inspire the word.

What then can this word have to say to politics? Must it ignore it? Or must it give it its blessing? Is it enough to learn the word of God well and then to spread it far and wide? There is no limit to these questions.

First of all, the word of God is essentially the proclamation of salvation. "It is not something that comes *from the outside* to man engaged in his scientific, technical and political occupations, in order to interrupt him or help him with them, but rather to reveal to him the inner meaning of his task in the world, the basis of his activity, and the projection into an unworldly and absolute future which this activity possesses."[21] The word the priest communicates is directed to man engaged in the task of building civilization. It impregnates every aspect of that task with meaning. And politics is one of the most important aspects of this task for it entails a direct relationship with the structuring of the common good.

Political action is not alien to the message of the Gospel,

[103]

and therefore the messenger of the Gospel's word must be concerned with it, keeping in mind, of course, that the Gospel cannot be reduced to a kind of earthly mysticism and, even less, be confused with a political action "program," as we shall show in good time.

For the proclamation of the Gospel, the priest must above all desacralize politics. What does that mean? Simply that he must assign politics its proper place within a teleological-eschatological perspective. He must de-absolutize politics, showing that it does not exhaust the task of faith, even though faith is not alien to it. The priest must situate the Church's teaching within the universal context of the Gospel message, at the risk of falling into a temporal messianism if only one aspect be stressed (in this case, the socio-political) and if everything that transcends earthly life is neglected.

Far from dissuading laymen from intervening in politics, he must spur them on, but without injecting some divine panacea into politics and without claiming any political stand in the Gospel truth, unless he wants to be guilty of propagating a secular religion, as we have already warned. The priest does not withdraw from the political arena, but works toward providing it with a foundation and its true meaning, by giving politics its proper place or restoring it to it, and by planting at its core the dimensions which should frame it: justice and peace. "It is in situating the Church's social teaching within the total dimensions of the Gospel . . . that the priest has the opportunity to make himself heard. If he makes this demanding effort, he will be less tempted to assume responsibilities proper to the layman, since he will realize that he is imparting something substantial to them, even if he himself is not involved in politics."[22]

Moreover, *Gaudium et Spes* clearly cautions laymen that they cannot expect concrete solutions to all the problems in the world today from priests. They themselves must assume their own responsibilities, illumined by the light emanating from the Word of God.

Seeing the danger behind making the Gospel message political, especially in the lower echelons of society, Cardinal Suhard wrote some twenty years ago: "The more manual the employment, the more estranged from the Church the worker lives. The Christian message is completely foreign to him. It is true that he preserves a certain nostalgia for the Gospel, but in his eyes the Church is a political power and her activity a selfish ploy."[23] Great, then, is the responsibility of those who by adulterating the genuine meaning of the message, are a cause of scandal and estrange from Christ and his Church those whom he loved most.

The word speaks to man in order to awaken his deepest vocation within him and to free him from the illusion that its fulness is to be found solely in the tasks of this world.

THE PRIEST'S SERVICE

In addition to being a minister of the Eucharist and of the word (or better, precisely because he is), the priest is the testimonial to the fact that all human activity is rooted in God; and by the same token, he is the safeguard for the teleological character of the person, called to the kingdom of God by way of this world (although it is not the kingdom itself, the world is the way to it). Here the Church-world polarity can be translated into a polarity between the earthly city and the City of God.

Between these two cities there is an eschatological relationship of continuity, but this is disrupted when man absolutizes one of the poles, the earthly city, and cuts it off from the other, the City of God. And the legitimate autonomy of the temporal is changed into a radical emancipation, thus losing the full meaning of the world as a work finalized in its own order, but opened out to a transcendence which gives it its reason for being.

This disruption of continuity is more dramatic today than ever, if we consider that in proportion to the advancement of rationality there is a retrogression of meaning, and that a dissolution of finalities corresponds to a greater understanding of instrumentality.[24] (A good example of this might be what is called the "literature of the absurd," "absurd" in this instance being understood as the lack of meaning and response to exasperating questions, posed by contemporary civilization with its whole technological and instrumental apparatus.)

It is indispensable, then, that there be someone who can overcome this discontinuity and reestablish the relationship. For this, however, it is necessary to be at a certain "distance" from the world, which is the only way not to lose sight of the perspective of the ultimate end, obscured by the intermediate ends' claim to "ultimateness."

This someone should be the priest, and his service is to remind mankind, by means of the word nourished by the Eucharist, that the kingdom of God is not attained merely by worldly efforts, even though these contribute toward preparing for it. But this "distance" that the priest must keep does not take him from the world. It places him at its very heart, although in a different way. The priest is *in* the world in a special manner and his commitment is more radical than any other because it is eschatological. It constitutes the utmost *response* to a vacillating ethic bereft of solid ground and a false ethics (closed humanism) which deforms man by failing to acknowledge his transcendent vocation. ". . . The priest in the world will always be the adversary . . . He will never be forgiven for constantly calling upon someone who was thought to have been eliminated forever."[25] Thus, the priest is the pre-eminent *response,* the man of battle, but as we shall see later, his weapons are an invitation to peace.

"The problem of the priest is inherent in his function: to be leaven in the dough is a task at once paradoxical and delicate, because it involves the bringing together of contraries. In order to be leaven, the priest must be close, very close to men. Leaven which is placed but a fraction of an inch from the dough, can have effect. But if the leaven loses its own character, that is, if it loses its capacity to 'go against' the dough, it will not cause it to rise. . . ."[26] A priest engaged in politics will never become leaven, nor will the priest who stands aloof from it. "Under certain aspects," different from the world, but *in* the world, that is the position of the priest.

Man's fascination with his own accomplishments in the field of science and technology fills him with such satisfaction that he seems to leave no place for God. In the hyper-developed plane of politics, something similar happens. God seemingly has no place in political activity because it is cut off from its teleological dimension, is self-sufficient, and capable of creating the structural conditions which bring man to his fulfilment: a Promethean mirage that claims to complete and perfect the universe on its own efforts alone.

It is against this illusion that the priest must fight by showing the relativeness of politics. But he must not overlook its essential importance in shaping a world that is open to transcendence. "His mission is to preserve the contingent as it is, and also to uncover in all initiatives the 'open door' spoken of by Paul, in order to give it its full meaning of existence in the faith."[27]

Yet the fact that a priest is not bound to a particular political regime does not mean that he is indifferent to any regime whatsoever. On the contrary, he must raise his prophetic voice against regimes that turn man into just one more factor within the dynamic of civilization. Giving politics its correct meaning and working to give it a foundation also involve criticizing it, struggling so that it may open to the discovery of its own meaning.

"Within the Church (the priest) will have the mission of

opening up horizons and fostering freedom whereby each man can become receptive to the faith. If Christians tend to withdraw and to escape the world, if like any other group of men they look with misgivings to the 'outside,' and want to preserve for themselves alone the security of their salvation, the priest will then have to denounce this narrowing of vision and generosity . . . and proclaim anew that Christ came to break down all the barriers that divide men . . . If Christians who are ardent advocates of an 'ideology' (even one 'inspired' within Christianity) tend to confuse it with the Gospel of Christ and to impose it through pressure, political maneuver or frontal attack, the priest will have to be on his guard against this temptation and remind everyone that without freedom there is no worthwhile Christianity."[28] If politics is a barrier that divides men, the priest must bring it back to its real meaning and purge it of all divisive hatreds. Here, once again, we present the priest as a sign of unity, and even more, as a guarantee of freedom without which man cannot respond to God.

How could the priest discharge this critical-prophetic function if he himself were committed to political action? By what mysterious duplication of his person? We leave the question unanswered.

THE PRIEST'S COURSE OF ACTION

Gaudium et Spes states that the ways and means of building the world are different from the ways and means proper to the Gospel (no. 76, par. 4). *L'Action populaire* sheds some clarification on this statement: "Now, it is not a question . . . of the *general* problem of relations between religious society and political community . . . but of the particular attitude to be adopted by apostles and pastors, those who are dedicated to the ministry of God's word. Not merely because of the distinction between two societies and to prevent the Church's usurping the prerogatives of political society, but also to testify to the ultimate meaning of human destiny and of the love of God, the Church's ministers and all apostles must act, utilizing means other than those of political life. They will have to be especially careful never to violate and always respect the other's freedom. They will choose poverty over wealth, humility over honor."[29]

These lines, especially the last ones, clearly flow from the kenotic character of Christ's Church, and as well make primary the distance between priesthood and politics, between Church and power. To fulfil his mission, the priest must eschew power and force which are means proper to politics: "His weapon is not the passion of pride nor brute force, but the humility of the Gospel and the folly of the cross."[30]

In this regard Max Weber's words are quite pertinent: "The great virtuosos of love for neighbor and unworldly welfare, whether of Nazareth or Assisi . . . did not work with political means, with force. Their 'kingdom was not of this world,' despite the fact of their past and present effectiveness in it . . . He who seeks the salvation of his soul and those of others, let him not seek it along the path of politics. Its tasks, which are quite different, can only be accomplished through force. The genius or daimon of politics lives in internal tension with the god of love, including the Christian God in his ecclesiastical configuration, and this tension can be converted at any moment into an insoluble conflict."[31]

Despite the latent belittlement of politics in the foregoing paragraph, there is an obvious tension between love and the political struggle, a tension which the priest must alleviate, not by getting into politics, but by reminding politics of its real significance: the attainment of peace and justice among men and the structuring of a more human world which would permit man's opening up to God and which would not cut off this opening at its root. The priest must confront politics in order to strip it of its aggressive character, which ghettoizes and subjugates men to a purpose that has become absolutized.

As we said, this mission of the priest demands of him a certain distancing from the world so that he can carry on the work to which the Lord is calling him *within* the people of God, *within* mankind, and not at the fringes. This apartness, like the nature of his mission, is translated into the need to find a certain life style which will take into account the distinction between the earthly city and the kingdom of God,[32] and witness to the fact that God alone is absolute and necessary and that in him all human endeavor finds its goal.

This life-style will not consist in "inventing or *choosing* a given aspect within the priesthood, which would seem better adapted to our contemporaries. For all priests, no matter what the means or the periods under consideration, it will consist in their remaining faithful to what Jesus Christ was: 'the Mediator' of salvation."[33] Evidently, this mediation of salvation can be clothed in different modalities which in no way affect its essence. The priest workers, for instance, lived their mediation in a special way (prescinding from whether they were right or not) without adulterating their salvific ministry.

The problem is rooted in what Manaranche[34] calls the "professional ailment" inherent in every occupation. In the present instance, the ailment is found between the priest's life and function. This apparent antinomy between life and function is partly divested of its aspect of mutual incompatibility by Manaranche when he recognizes in today's priests the twelve apostles called by Christ. With the apostles, their task and the way it was to be carried out could not be separated: ". . . delegated by Christ to proclaim Christ himself, the apostle must identify himself with Christ. Thus, the close union with the person is included in the function."[35] In this regard, we must recall the identification brought about in the mystery of the Eucharist, when the priest says "this is my body . . ."

This life style, as we pointed out in the beginning, is a source of anguish for many priests. It is manifested in certain "ruptures" with or renunciations of other forms of human productivity which are good in themselves. Among them we find politics. The priest gives up certain activities in order to be able to sanctify them, to make them things of God (which should not be confused with the sacralization of politics which we have rejected). "Such an attitude implies no reticence toward the worthiness and common necessity of political action for the good of the unity and personal equilibrium of men. Nor does the celibate need to justify himself by attempting to de-emphasize the value of human love and its specific manifestations. On the contrary, in both cases, something good and important is given up, and by this very act of self-denial the thing given up takes on great value because it points up the *dépassement* towards which the priest is striving and the reward promised him by God."[36]

Obviously, this renunciation does not mean the priest's estrangement from politics, but rather his avoidance of a militant political commitment. Still remaining is his more radical and thorough priestly commitment to the political.

But, in addition to these reasons justifying a renunciation of formal political action, there are others of a quite different nature such as reasons of efficacy and competence. We shall briefly analyze them.

We can begin with a simple verification. In every society, each man has the duty to concern himself with those for whom he is most immediately responsible. This is not only a moral duty. The civil laws themselves forbid the simultaneous exercise of certain activities, as in France, for instance, with the incompatibility of being a parliamentary representative and a union representative at the same time, or, as in most countries, the incompatibility between political action and military service. This necessary role distinction may also be applied to the priest, not by civil law of course, but by a principle of consistency acknowledged by the Church herself.

What happens, then, if a priest assumes a political role in addition to his own proper function? Above all, politics itself runs a great risk, one which is very common in Latin America: the adulteration or "profanation" of politics. Religious categories leave their true orbit and begin to lead the secular world. It can be sustained that this undue projection of the specifically religious onto the political field is a real adulteration of the secular which is shown, for example, in the political concept of the State as Providence. The functional irrationality and the confusion of roles to which this leads are obvious. Let the politician take care lest this intrusion take place!

Needless to say, on the other hand, we come back to the aberration, so often condemned, of a neoclericalism which, this time, is supported by specious arguments. Indeed, people say that, through political action, the priest can succeed in regaining his place in a society which rejects the ministry of the word and the service of theological thought and that at the same time the political commitment of the Church permits her to show her efficacy in the face of the problems of the modern world.

However, is it certain that society rejects the service of the priest on principle or out of prejudice? It would seem not. What it does reject, and quite rightly, is the kind of priest who since he is involved in politics rejects his ministry or prostitutes it by the use of illegitimate means, thereby rendering it ineffective. What it rejects is nothing else but the reflection of the very rejection by the "political" priest of those who do not share his views. Even though this rejection on the priest's part be completely unconscious, psychologically he cannot be open to all the faithful (discounting the fact that he may not have time to do so), and they in turn do not have the psychological freedom necessary to respond to him. Congar's words in this respect are worthy of consideration: "The priest must be the priest of all. He must try to conduct himself in such a way that no man can have an objectively valid motive for not asking him to hear his confession. The Church is more than a dimension or an animation of the world."[37]

In respect to efficacy, it would we well to ask: "Efficacy for what?" If it is to bring the re-activated word of the faith to the modern world and to discover in it the sense of that faith, there is no problem. But if it is to set up a "Christian political system," a power system in which the faith would be something anachronistic and harmful, it must be flatly rejected. Apostolic efficacy is something quite different from political activism.

The danger for religion is no less and has been seen throughout this work. Here too there is an adulteration of the priestly ministry, but this time through the projection of political programs into the religious sphere. The phantom of clericalism rears its head once more: spiritual influence in the service of politics with all the consequences pointed out above.

Father Marcus, a theologian from *Mission de France,* clearly points out the danger: "Priests must keep themselves aloof from commitments that would risk seriously affecting their pastoral relationship with believers and non-believers. A case in point would be, for instance, if a priest should involve himself in an enterprise, a movement, a political party, a leadership which might rightly bring down on him the accusation that he has put his spiritual authority (conferred on him by his concrete responsibility in the Church) at the service of a cause to which the Christian need not bind himself."[38]

This is not all. By the very nature of his ministry, the priest has no experience in politics and his viewpoint on politics is not the same as that of the "professional" politician.[39] This results in his becoming easy prey to clever politicians who want to use him for party interests, capitalizing on his status as an "inspirer of communities." This intrusion into areas that are foreign to his own competence also explains society's rejection.

"It is well that the priest be convinced and manifest throughout his state of life that he does not expect the progress of his ministry and of the kingdom to be brought about by human means, and even less by political pressure. The temptation to think that one can make more rapid progress by using human means is strong for him. And there is almost inevitable confusion in men's minds when he actively devotes himself to political action, and when he furthermore exercises a leadership responsibility or one that comes close to it in the political city."[40]

The priest must guide and enlighten Christians in their search for a just political structure. He must arrive at the doctrinal moment—properly understood—and leave it up to the laity to take the responsibility and the initiative of political action, remaining free to support their "structuring" with his constructive criticism. Thus, he will avoid playing "layman," as the Council warns, of course in other words.

"Like Christ, the priest will experience the temptation of the desert. Like him, the tempter will ask that 'the stones be changed into bread' and will propose submitting to his rule 'all the kingdoms of the earth.' Satan will insidiously try to persuade him that in virtue of his power, he is to be the artisan of progress on earth, and consequently, the defender of established regimes, or, as the case may be, the champion of revolutionary causes."[41] In the heart of a society in turmoil, the priest must keep ever in mind the danger of temporal messianism and remember that as one sent by Christ his "kingdom is not of this world." Christ in the desert refused to build the kingdom based on the prior satisfaction of human needs, however legitimate, or by means of human glory or political power. "No servant is greater than his master, nor is one who is sent greater than he who sent him . . ." (John 13, 16). The priest must eschew any Promethean attitude which is too frequently linked with his own personal ambitions.

In this sense, Manaranche[42] makes three "general considerations" which might more properly be called "counsels." In the first place, he maintains, the priest must "de-emotionalize and relativize his national problem" and also his personal situation. That is to say, he must avoid clerical chauvinism and closed individualism: "It is now no longer I that live, but Christ lives in me." (Galatians 2, 20). From this is derived Manaranche's second observation: there is a narcissism in the priest when he looks at his "situation without any theological reference to his mission. . . . He will never escape the crucial question: a priest OF whom and FOR WHOM." The third "consideration-counsel" holds that the priest "should not isolate himself in his search without the opinion and consent of other Christians, as if he were capable alone of resolving his problem independently from this people of God for whom he is made a priest and who have the right to present their views on the issues. If he does this, he will fall once again into that abhorrent clericalism which he has many a reason to wish to eschew."

As we can see, the danger of clericalism appears again and again from different viewpoints, and underlying this, as its counterpart, is the opposite danger: "angelism," the priest who moves along *on the sidelines* of men with his eyes raised to the kingdom, his ears deaf to human anguish.

The true dimension of the priest's commitment in politics is found, as we have tried to show in the preceding pages, in the affirmation of a solidarity and not in the extremes of a negative polarity such as clericalism or angelism.

NOTES

1. Roger Heckel, S.J., "Le Prêtre et la Politique," *Cahiers d'Action Religieuse et Sociale,* CERAS, no. 484 (Nov. 15, 1968), no. 486 (Dec. 15, 1968), no. 488 (Jan. 15, 1969), no. 489 (Feb. 1, 1970) and Manaranche, *op. cit.,* "Le Ministère Sacerdotal," pp. 229-237.

2. Weber, *El político y el científico, op. cit.,* p. 93.

3. The problem will be different for one who is a professional, married, and the father of a family and would receive the sacrament of orders and carry on a eucharistic function.

4. Manaranche, "Je réponds a l'enquête sur le prêtre," *Cahiers d'Action Religieuse et Sociale,* CERAS, no. 495 (May 1, 1969) 258.

5. According to the more than ambiguous expression used by Schillebeeckx in "The Church and Mankind," *art. cit.,* p. 81.

6. The translation is of the French *engagement,* in Spanish *compromiso,* hence commitment, involvement.

7. Chavasse, *Eglise et Apostolat, op. cit.,* p. 157.

8. Manaranche, "Le Prêtre," *Cahiers d'Action Religieuse et Sociale,* CERAS, no. 15 (November, 1965) 637.

9. Chavasse, *op. cit.,* pp. 201-202.

10. Manaranche, "Le Prêtre," *loc cit.*

11. Rahner, *Mission and Grace,* II (New York: Sheed and Ward, 1964), pp. 20-21.

12. Chavasse, *op. cit.,* p. 114.

13. Of course, we are not holding that this is the sole manner of communication by man with God and it is clear that the priest is not the exclusive mediator.

14. Otto Semmelroth, "The Priestly People of God and its Official Ministers," Concilium XXXI (New York: Paulist Press, 1968), p. 100.

15. Manaranche, "Le Prêtre," *op. cit.,* p. 631 (note).

16. Heckel, "Le Prêtre et la politique," *art. cit.,* no. 488, pp. 59, 60.

17. Manaranche, *Y-a-t-il une éthique sociale chretienne?, op. cit.,* p. 233.

18. Rahner, *Mission and Grace, op. cit.,* p. 44.

19. Manaranche, *Y-a-t-il une éthique . . . , op. cit.,* p. 237.

20. Manuel Ossa, S.J., "El Sacerdote y el mundo de hoy," *Teologia y Vida* (Santiago) 7, (October-December, 1966), 280.

21. *Ibid.*

22. Heckel, *art cit.,* no. 488, p. 62.

23. Emmanuel Cardinal Suhard, "El Sacerdote en el Mundo," in *Dios, Iglesia, Sacerdote* (Madrid: Rialp, 1961), p. 271.

24. *Cf.* Ricoeur, "Prévision économique et choix éthique," *Esprit* (February, 1966) 186-189.

25. Suhard, *op. cit.,* p. 298.

26. Léon-Joseph Cardinal Suenens, *Co-responsibility in the Church* (New York: Herder and Herder, 1968), pp. 108-109.

27. Juan de Castro, "La fe del sacerdote en el mundo," *Teologia y Vida* (Santiago) 7 (October-December 1966) 299.

28. Ossa, *art. cit.,* pp. 280-281.

29. *"Gaudium et Spes," Notes par l'Action Populaire, op. cit.,* note 163, p. 306.

30. Suhard, *op. cit.,* p. 299.

31. Weber, *op. cit.,* pp. 173-174.

32. "Priests cannot be ministers of Christ unless they are witnesses and dispensers of a life other than this earthly one. But they cannot be of service to men if they remain strangers to the life and conditions of men" (Vatican II, *Presbyterorum ordinis,* 3).

33. Suhard, *op. cit.,* pp. 270-271.

34. Manaranche, "Le Prêtre," *art. cit.*, p. 674.

35. *Ibid.*, p. 630.

36. Heckel, *art. cit.*, no. 489, p. 89.

37. Congar, *Au milieu del orages,* (Paris: Cerf, 1969), p. 48.

38. E. Marcus, "Les Prêtres après Vatican II," in *Prêtres et Pasteurs,* Eglises en dialogue 6 (Paris: Mame, 1968), pp. 147-148. (Cited by Congar, *op. cit.*, p. 49).

39. Of course, this does not exclude the priest's obligation to be politically formed and informed.

40. Heckel, *art. cit.*, p. 94.

41. Suhard, *op. cit.*, p. 279.

42. Manaranche, *Y-a-t-il une éthique . . .* , *op. cit.*, p. 236.